Academic Writing and Referencing for your
Nursing Degree

CRITICAL STUDY SKILLS

Critical Study Skills for Nursing Students

Our new series of study skills texts for nursing and other health professional students has four key titles to help you succeed at your degree:

Studying for your Nursing Degree

Academic Writing and Referencing for your Nursing Degree

Critical Thinking Skills for your Nursing Degree

Communication Skills for your Nursing Degree

Register with **Critical Publishing** to:

- be the first to know about forthcoming nursing titles;
- find out more about our new series;
- sign up for our regular newsletter for special offers, discount codes and more.

Visit our website at:  **www.criticalpublishing.com**

Our titles are also available in a range of electronic formats. To order please go to our website www.criticalpublishing.com or contact our distributor NBN International by telephoning 01752 202301 or emailing orders@nbninternational.com.

Academic Writing and Referencing for your **Nursing Degree**

JANE BOTTOMLEY AND STEVEN PRYJMACHUK

First published in 2017 by Critical Publishing Ltd

British Library Cataloguing in Publication Data
A CIP record for this book is available from the British Library

ISBN: 978-1-911106-95-1

This book is also available in the following e-book formats:

MOBI: 978-1-911106-96-8
EPUB: 978-1-911106-97-5
Adobe e-book reader: 978-1-911106-98-2

Text and cover design by Out of House Limited
Project management by Out of House Publishing
Print managed and manufactured by Jellyfish Solutions

Critical Publishing
3 Connaught Road
St Albans
AL3 5RX
www.criticalpublishing.com

Contents

Acknowledgements

We would like to thank the many university and nursing students who have inspired us to write these books. Special thanks are due to Anita Gill. Our appreciation also goes to Andrew Drummond and Maureen Finn for their comments on specific parts of the manuscript.

Jane Bottomley and Steven Pryjmachuk

Meet the authors

Jane Bottomley

is a Senior Language Tutor at the University of Manchester and a Senior Fellow of the British Association of Lecturers in English for Academic Purposes (BALEAP). She has helped students from a wide range of disciplines to improve their academic skills and achieve their study goals. She has previously published on scientific writing.

Steven Pryjmachuk

is Professor of Mental Health Nursing Education in the School of Health Science's Division of Nursing, Midwifery and Social Work at the University of Manchester and a Senior Fellow of the Higher Education Academy. His teaching, clinical and research work has centred largely on supporting and facilitating individuals – be they students, patients or colleagues – to develop, learn or care independently.

Introduction

Academic Writing and Referencing is the second book in the *Critical Study Skills for Nurses* series. The *Critical Study Skills for Nurses* series supports student nurses, midwives and health professionals as they embark on their undergraduate degree programmes. It is aimed at all student nurses, including those who have come to university straight from A levels, and those who have travelled a different route, perhaps returning to education after working or raising a family. The books will be of use both to students from the UK, and international students who are preparing to study in a new culture – and perhaps in a second language. The books also include guidance for students with specific learning difficulties.

Academic Writing and Referencing provides you with the knowledge, language, skills and strategies that you need in order to develop your academic writing skills and succeed in writing assignments. It introduces you to typical nursing writing assignments, and explores important areas such as the writing process, coherence, referring to sources, academic style and grammatical accuracy. It helps you to develop important skills such as planning and editing. It reflects the centrality of criticality in writing by referring to it throughout the different chapters, and shows how it is achieved through a multi-layered approach, including development of stance and argument, choice of language, and considered reference to sources. The book also helps you to prepare your work to a professional standard for submission.

Between them, the authors have many years' experience of both nursing practice and education, and academic study skills. All the information, text extracts and activities in the book have a clear nursing focus and are often directly linked to the **Nursing and Midwifery Council's Code**. There is also reference to relevant institutional bodies, books and journals throughout.

The many activities in the book include reflections, case studies, top tips, checklists and tasks. There are also advanced skills sections, which highlight particular knowledge and skills that you will need towards the end of your degree programme – or perhaps if you go on to postgraduate study. The activities often require you to work things out and discover things for yourself, a learning technique which is commonly used in universities. For many activities, there is no right or wrong answer – they might simply require you to reflect on your experience or situations you are likely to encounter at university; for tasks which require a particular response, there is an answer key at the back of the book.

These special features throughout the book are clearly signalled by icons to help you recognise them:

  Learning outcomes;

  Quick quiz or example exam questions/assessment tasks;

  Reflection (a reflective task or activity);

  Task;

  Case studies;

  Top tips;

  Checklist;

  Advanced skills information;

 Answer provided at the back of the book.

Students with limited experience of academic life in the UK will find it helpful to work through the book systematically; more experienced students may wish to 'dip in and out' of the book. Whichever approach you adopt, handy **cross references** signalled in the margins will help you quickly find the information that you need to focus on or revisit.

There are four appendices at the back of the book which you can consult as you work through the text.

We hope that this book will help you to develop as an academic writer and to become a confident member of your academic writing community. We hope it will help you to achieve your goals and produce written work to the very best of your abilities.

A note on terminology

In the context of this book, the term 'nursing' should be taken to include 'nursing, midwifery and the allied health professions', wherever this is not explicitly stated.

Chapter 1
Academic writing:
text, process and criticality

There are many challenges facing you as you embark on your nursing degree. You need to assimilate a great deal of information, and engage in new ideas and intellectual processes. What's more, you need to become proficient in academic writing, and learn how to produce the different types of text that are common in nursing.

Academic writing is central to your university studies, as written assignments and exams will be one of the main ways in which you are assessed. This chapter explores the nature of academic writing in universities, and helps you to develop an effective, systematic approach to the academic writing process. All assignments are different, and universities vary slightly in terms of the types of writing assignments they employ. This chapter focuses on some general principles which can be applied to most academic writing, including what it means to write 'critically'. It also discusses some of the most common features of individual text types in your discipline, with a particular focus on the critical essay.

Academic writing at university: a new start?

Nursing students in the UK come from a range of backgrounds: some come straight from A levels (or Scottish Highers); some have been away from formal education for some time, maybe working and/or bringing up a family; some come from other countries to study in the UK. This means that students starting university differ in terms of their writing abilities, their experience of academic writing, and how confident they feel about tackling written assessments.

So where do you fit in?

You may be feeling confident. You may be relishing the prospect of writing your first assignment, seeing it as an exciting opportunity to explore your subject and demonstrate your knowledge and ideas. You may be able to draw on recent experience of academic writing and positive feedback from teachers.

Conversely, you may be feeling rather apprehensive about your first written assignment. Like many students, you perhaps see academic writing as one of the most difficult challenges of university life. There are a number of reasons why you may be feeling apprehensive. You might not have much experience of academic writing. Or maybe you do have experience, but it might have been a long time ago, or in your mother tongue, not English. You may have struggled with writing in the past and received some negative comments from teachers. All of these things can make the prospect of that first written assignment rather daunting.

CROSS REFERENCE

Chapter 2, Coherent texts and arguments, Editing and redrafting for coherence, The truth about writing!

When starting to write at university, it is important for students to draw on any strengths they have in terms of ability and experience. But it is also important for all students to identify aspects of their writing which can be improved on. At university, you are part of a **writing community**, comprised of students, lecturers and researchers, and all members of that community are constantly striving to improve as writers, even those who publish in journals and books.

You should commit yourself to improving as a writer throughout your degree programme, and beyond, in your professional life. It is not a question of achieving perfection; it is rather a case of committing yourself to making many small improvements over time, and not giving up when faced with a disappointment or hurdle. University lecturers see many students develop into very good writers after a shaky start. What these students have in common is a positive attitude, an ability to reflect on and critically assess their own work, and a willingness to seek and act on advice.

This book will support you in your development as a writer by helping you to approach writing in a systematic way. It will enable you to:

- analyse and respond to writing tasks;
- plan and structure your writing effectively;
- achieve clarity and coherence in your writing;
- produce writing which is accurate and academic in style;
- write critically in assignments;
- use and reference sources appropriately;
- prepare assignments to a high professional standard for submission.

This chapter sets you on your way by exploring the context of academic writing at university and providing guidance on how to approach writing assignments on your nursing degree.

Academic writing for nursing undergraduates

CROSS REFERENCE

Communication Skills

Undergraduate nurses may be asked to produce a number of different types of academic writing, including essays, written reflections, exams, reports, reviews of journal articles, and dissertations. This chapter sets out a general approach to academic writing that will help you with all types of assignments. It also provides specific information on essays, written reflections, exams and dissertations. Advice on practical writing tasks in nursing is provided in *Communication Skills for your Nursing Degree*.

- **Essays**. There are different types of essays. The main one, sometimes called a 'critical' or 'analytical' essay, requires you to explore a particular topic in depth, usually in response to a question or statement, and to explain your own viewpoint, or 'stance', supported by arguments and evidence. A 'reflective' essay requires you to analyse and evaluate a particular experience, explaining its impact on your understanding and future practice.
- **Written reflections**. Nurses are often required to produce short written reflections on their experience in practice, usually as part of a **professional portfolio**.
- **Exams**. In exams, you may be required to provide short or long written responses to questions or statements. These are usually designed to demonstrate that you have assimilated and understood the core work covered in a particular module. They may require you to recall

factual information and/or to explain and support your viewpoint on a particular issue you have examined as part of your studies.

- **Dissertations**. A dissertation is a long evidence-based or research-focused essay written in the final year of your undergraduate studies.

Each of these types of academic writing will be discussed in more detail later in the chapter.

The writing process

Writing is a process and it involves a number of stages, including:

- 'unpacking' (analysing and understanding) the writing task and any guidelines provided;
- drawing up a provisional plan/outline;
- identifying relevant material that you need to read;
- reading and gathering information;
- drafting, redrafting, editing;
- revisiting and reworking your plan/outline;
- formatting your text;
- double-checking the assessment guidelines;
- proofreading.

It is important to fully engage with the writing process, and to understand that the *writing process* is part of the *learning* process. Writing is not just a question of getting fully formed thoughts down on paper (apart from in exams); it is a way of *clarifying your thinking* on a particular topic. Woodford (1967) put this nicely many years ago:

> *The power of writing as an aid in thinking is not often appreciated. Everyone knows that someone who writes successfully gets his thoughts completely in order before he publishes. But it is seldom pointed out that the very act of writing can help to clarify thinking. Put down woolly thoughts on paper, and their wooliness is immediately exposed.*

(p 744)

Top tips

Engaging with the writing process

1) Try to develop good writing habits. Write little and often, especially if you have been away from formal education for a while.
2) Adopt a write-read-edit-read approach to writing (discussed in Chapter 2). When you stop to read what you have written, stand back from the text. Put yourself in the reader's shoes and make sure that everything hangs together, makes sense, and flows smoothly.
3) Try to get some feedback during the writing process. You may have the opportunity to submit a first draft to a lecturer, or you could ask a fellow student to read something and give feedback. If you do ask a friend or fellow student, it's a good idea to ask them to *summarise* what they think you are trying to say. If you only ask them if they understand what you have written, they may just say yes to be polite!

Your exact approach to the writing process will depend on the particular context of the assignment and your individual way of working, but some essential aspects of the writing process are discussed in the following sections.

Approaching a writing assignment

A writer needs an audience, a purpose, and a strategy, and these things are interconnected (Swales and Feak, 2012, p 10). When approaching a writing assignment, ask yourself:

- Who is reading my work? (your audience)

CROSS REFERENCE

Studying for your Nursing Degree, Chapter 6, Assessment

CROSS REFERENCE

Chapter 2, Coherent texts and arguments, Editing and redrafting for coherence

3

- Why am I writing? (your purpose)
- How will I achieve my purpose? (your strategy)

CROSS
REFERENCE

Analysing
a writing
assignment

Your purpose is to meet the requirements of the assignment, and satisfy the needs and expectations of a particular reader. To determine your purpose, you need to analyse the wording of the task or question carefully. It may specify certain aspects of the topic that you should cover, and the verbs it uses, such as 'describe', 'explain', or 'evaluate', will determine how you treat this content. However, notwithstanding these specifications, there is no single 'right answer': different students will respond to a task in different ways. Your individual approach and strategy will determine:

CROSS
REFERENCE

Appendix 3,
Key phrases in
assignments

- the selection of content (information, arguments, evidence etc);
- the way this content is structured and organised.

The person reading your essay must be able to discern *why* you have included particular content and organised your essay in the way that you have.

The question of the 'reader' is a tricky one. Of course, the actual human being reading your assignment is your university lecturer – probably the one who set the task and taught the module. However, lecturers often ask (or expect) you to imagine a 'hypothetical' or 'target' reader. This is usually someone with a similar level of knowledge to your own, or someone with a similar level of education but who is not an expert in nursing. Lecturers want you to write for such a reader because they want you to *demonstrate* your understanding, and you cannot do this if you assume too much knowledge on the part of the reader. It is not uncommon to ask a student about something which is unclear in their essay, only to have them explain that 'the lecturer already knows this'! But this is not the point. The lecturer wants to know that *you* know this, and that you can explain it to other people, including non-experts, in a clear way. Always ask yourself:

CROSS
REFERENCE

Chapter 2,
Coherent
texts and
arguments,
Editing and
redrafting for
coherence;
Developing
a coherent
argument and
expressing
criticality

- What can the target reader be expected to know?
- What does the target reader need me to explain?

A good writer anticipates the reader's questions, and does not ask them to guess, fill in gaps, or work out how one thing relates to another.

Analysing a writing assignment

CROSS
REFERENCE

Appendix 3,
Key phrases in
assignments

One of the most common – and perhaps surprising – reasons for low marks in written assessments is the failure on the part of the student to read the assignment title or question thoroughly enough. A student may go on to produce something which is interesting and of a good standard, but if they do not directly address the specific task, they will not meet the actual requirements of the assignment and so will end up failing. It is therefore essential to start any assignment by carefully analysing the assignment title or question.

You should read the title or question several times to 'unpack' it and get absolutely clear in your mind what is expected of you. It is helpful to highlight **key terms**, including verbs commonly occurring in academic assignments such as 'assess', 'discuss', and 'compare and contrast'.

CROSS
REFERENCE

*Studying for
your Nursing
Degree*,
Chapter 6,
Assessment,
Feedback on
academic
work

Assignments usually come with a set of assessment **guidelines** and marking **descriptors** detailing the various criteria that you need to meet in order to achieve success. These criteria relate to areas such as:

- task achievement;
- content and organisation;
- relevance to nursing practice;
- writing style;
- referencing.

Be sure to read and digest these guidelines and descriptors as they are the very same ones that assessors will use to mark your work.

Task

Unpacking essay titles and questions

Look at the essay titles below. What are the key terms? What are you expected to do in your essay? What will be your purpose in writing? What type of content and organisation could help you to achieve this purpose? (Make some notes before you look at the model analyses provided.)

A

Given the many factors that might influence the health of an individual, consider the question: 'Can nurses really influence the health of others?'

B

'The core skill of nursing is the ability to communicate.' Using appropriate evidence, explore the arguments for and against this proposition.

Discussion: unpacking essay titles and questions

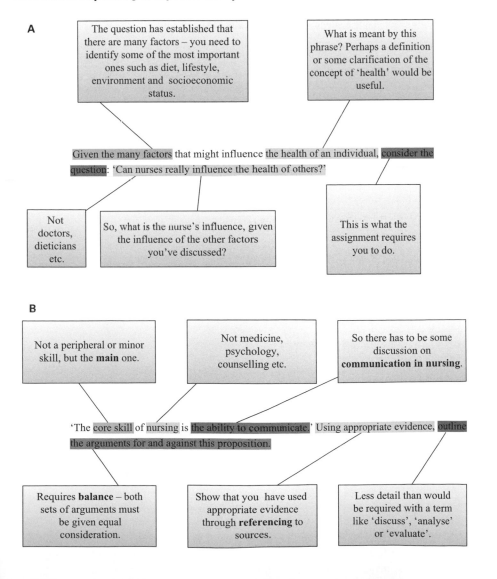

Planning

CROSS
REFERENCE

Chapter 5,
Preparing
your work for
submission,
Editing and
proofreading
your final text

Always begin an assignment by considering the constraints of the task: how long it should be and how long you have to write it. You could then draw up a provisional schedule which allocates time to the various sub-tasks. This schedule should leave sufficient time for you to read through and proofread the whole text several times before submitting.

A good piece of writing starts with a good plan or 'outline'. This should be primarily based on your analysis, or 'unpacking', of the task, but it should evolve as you engage in the reading and writing process. Your outline is therefore much more than a list of items related to the assignment topic: it is a developing conceptual representation of your response to the task. For example, in relation to the essay titles analysed above, your outline would reflect your position, or 'stance', in relation to the given topic, ie:

CROSS
REFERENCE

Writing
critically

- A: the extent to which you believe, supported by your investigation of the arguments and evidence, that nurses can influence the health of others
- B: your assessment of the evidence you find to support or challenge the main proposition that communication is the core skill of nursing

An outline should identify key sections of the text (with possible subheadings), and, in a critical essay, the arguments and evidence that would feature in each one.

CROSS
REFERENCE

Chapter 2,
Coherent
texts and
arguments,
Planning for
coherence

As discussed earlier in this chapter, different students will approach the same task in different ways. Sometimes an essay title will specify broad organisational requirements. For example, in B above, you are asked to 'outline the arguments for and against' the proposition. However, you might decide either to look at all the 'for' arguments in the first half of the essay and all the 'against' arguments in the second half, or, alternatively, to examine the proposition from both angles with reference to a series of different areas of nursing. In other essays, you may have more leeway. One common approach is to examine different positions one by one, finally making a case for the one which the majority of the evidence seems to support. Another approach is to make a strong case for one particular position right from the start, while acknowledging and examining alternative (but in your view, weaker) viewpoints along the way.

Top tips

Aligning your outline and the task requirements

When your outline is well developed, go back to your initial analysis of the task to make sure that you have addressed all the points that you originally highlighted, and that you have achieved the required balance in your response.

CROSS
REFERENCE

Studying for
your Nursing
Degree,
Chapter 4,
Critical
thinking,
Applying and
developing
your critical
thinking skills;
Chapter 5,
Academic
resources:
technology
and the library,
The university
library

Reading and information gathering

Most academic writing assignments require you to read about a particular topic and use scholarly sources to inform your ideas. A good place to start the reading for an assignment is your lecture notes. These will provide an overview of the topic, and they will probably include links to some relevant literature, such as key chapters from core textbooks, and important journal articles, case studies, official reports etc. At the beginning of your studies, lecturers will tend to direct you to relevant sources in this way, but as you progress through your degree, you will be expected to explore the literature more widely and independently. As you develop these research skills, you will be increasingly assessed on your ability to find and select sources, and to use your critical judgement to assess their relevance and credibility. Lecturers will expect you to refer both to sources which support your position on a topic, and sources which challenge it.

Academic texts can be long and difficult to read because of the technical content, much of which may be new to you. It is essential that you devote enough time to reading, but it is also important that you develop effective reading strategies so that you use that time efficiently. When you approach a book, chapter or journal article, first adopt a 'global' approach, ie identify:

- what you expect to find out from it, and how these things relate to your assignment;
- the main message (the author's purpose in writing), and how this relates to your assignment;
- the main points made by the author(s), and how they relate to the main message of the article, and to your assignment.

As you think about how what you are reading relates to the assignment in hand, you might use highlighting, annotations, or note-taking to reflect this. You should also mark or make a note of parts of the text that you think you may need to read more closely at some stage.

Top tips

Strategies for effective reading

1) Use features such as contents pages, indices, abstracts, introductions and conclusions to help you assess the relevance of a book, chapter or article and find specific content.

2) Note how textbooks and journal articles on a particular topic are interrelated. Important books and articles are likely to be referenced by other scholars, and your initial reading may provide links to other sources that could be useful for your essay. This becomes more important as you progress in your studies.

3) You are likely to encounter unknown words in academic reading. Some of these might be subject-related technical terms, such as 'dopamine' or 'apnea', which you should familiarise yourself with; others may be formal words which are uncommon outside academic writing, such as 'analogous' or 'dichotomy'. If English is not your first language, there may be quite a number of words which are new to you. There is a limited amount of time you can spend reading, so you need to make decisions about how much time to spend investigating unknown non-technical words. Looking up every word you don't know will eat into your reading time and disrupt the reading process. What's more, it is unlikely that you will be able to remember all of these words in the future. Try using these two questions to determine whether or not you should look up a word:

- Does the word prevent you from understanding the general meaning?
- Is the word repeated a lot in this text or related texts?

If the answer to these questions is no, then attempt to guess the word using the context to help you, and read on; if the answer is yes, look up the word.

4) As you take notes, take care to make a note of the reference, including page numbers. It will waste a lot of time if you have to wade through all your sources again when you are compiling your list of references.

5) Try to paraphrase, ie take notes *in your own words*. This will benefit you in these ways:

- as you strive to express ideas in your own way, you will process them and get a good sense of how well you understand what you are reading;
- if you express things in your own words from the start, there is less of a risk of plagiarism in the final version of your assignment.

CROSS REFERENCE

Studying for your Nursing Degree, Chapter 4, Critical thinking, Active reading

CROSS REFERENCE

Chapter 3, Referring to sources

Advanced skills

Understanding research article introductions: the CARS model

You will be expected to read and refer to research articles throughout your studies, but as you progress, you will be increasingly expected to take the initiative in finding and selecting particular articles that are relevant to your assignments. The first thing you should look at when considering an article is the **abstract**. This will give you a good idea of whether the article is useful and relevant. If you then decide that you want to find out more, you should begin by looking closely at the **introduction**. This will be easier if you know what to look for. Article introductions typically move through a series of rhetorical stages, or 'moves', ie parts of a text designed to have a particular effect; this is known as the CARS (Creating a Research Space) model (Swales, 1990, p 141).

CROSS REFERENCE

Studying for your Nursing Degree, Chapter 3, Becoming a member of your academic and professional community, Academic phrasebank

- **Move 1** involves 'establishing a territory', ie showing that the research area is central or important. This is often achieved through a review of items of previous research in the area.

- **Move 2** involves 'establishing a niche', ie establishing an individual position in relation to the research previously conducted. This often means indicating a 'gap' in the research, by raising questions about or seeking to extend current knowledge in some way.

- **Move 3** involves 'occupying the niche'. This can be by outlining the nature or purposes of the current research, announcing principal findings, and/or indicating the structure of the paper.

Awareness of the CARS model, and other typical rhetorical patterns, can help you to read and understand difficult articles. Furthermore, understanding the language associated with these rhetorical features of academic writing can help you develop your own academic writing 'toolkit'. You can find many examples of useful phrases which 'move a text forward' in the Academic Phrasebank:

www.phrasebank.manchester.ac.uk/

Writing essentials

There are three things which are especially important in academic writing.

CROSS REFERENCE

Chapter 2, Coherent texts and arguments

1) **Relevance.** Be sure to make everything you write relevant to the task or question. If the relevance of a point is not immediately clear, then try to make it clear; if you cannot make it clear, leave it out. You will usually have a strict word count, so it is vital not to waste words on irrelevant material which cannot contribute to your mark.

2) **Coherence.** Lecturers often comment on the need for a piece of writing to be 'coherent', or deduct marks for 'lack of coherence'. To be coherent, a piece of writing must **make sense** to the reader. Coherence is tied up with issues discussed earlier, such as having a clear purpose and direction, and writing with a target reader in mind. It is also defined by clear organisation and expression. Coherent texts are *crafted*: they need careful planning and editing. The concept of coherence is examined in detail in Chapter 2.

CROSS REFERENCE

Chapter 2, Coherent texts and arguments, Developing a coherent argument and expressing criticality

3) **Criticality.** Most academic writing is 'critical' writing, ie it is analytical and evaluative, rather than just descriptive. This will be discussed below and in other chapters.

Writing critically

A basic requirement in assignments is to make it clear that you have understood important concepts, theories and arguments. In your first year of study, this level of intellectual engagement and understanding is sufficient to pass an assignment. However, as you progress through your nursing studies, you will be increasingly assessed on your ability to demonstrate that you have approached concepts, theories, arguments etc *critically*.

CROSS REFERENCE

Chapter 3, Referring to sources

Stance

Criticality is related to the idea of having a clear **voice** (Argent, 2017). This means having something to say, and being in possession of an independent **viewpoint** or **perspective** on a given topic. In the academic world, this is known as your **stance**, ie, your position in relation to the topic (what *you* think about it) and to the reader (what you want *them* to think about it). There are two questions to consider:

1) How can you explain your stance?

2) How can you justify your stance and persuade the reader that your stance is valid?

Consider the following essay title:

Discuss the value of health promotion in tackling alcohol misuse.

Many people would be prepared to offer an opinion on this topic without thinking about it too much: 'I suppose health promotion must do some good, otherwise governments wouldn't bother'; 'In my experience, people don't take a blind bit of notice of official health campaigns.' Or they may be reluctant to voice an opinion: 'It's not something I've really thought about.' But your lecturers are not interested in this kind of response; they are interested in a viewpoint that emerges from your *critical engagement* with information, evidence, ideas and debate in academic literature, in this case, the literature dedicated to the issue of health promotion as a way of tackling alcohol misuse. *After carefully analysing and evaluating the literature*, you may come to the conclusion that a) health promotion is of immense value in tackling alcohol misuse, b) health promotion has little impact on alcohol misuse, c) health promotion may have some value, but other factors may impact equally or more – you may perhaps remain undecided in the face of conflicting evidence. These thoughtful conclusions are very different from the casual opinions stated at the beginning of this paragraph.

Argument

To explain and justify your stance to the reader, you need to present an **argument**. An argument is a way of organising and expressing a viewpoint. It involves a process of **reasoning**, and, to be valid in the academic world, it must be based on solid, convincing **evidence**. This will partly emerge from your analysis and evaluation of the stance, arguments and conclusions of other scholars, and of the evidence they use as support, according to objective criteria (is the argument logical? Does it lead logically to their conclusions? Is the evidence sound? Does it support their claims?). You will need to compare alternative viewpoints and judge them according to the same criteria. It is on the basis of this analysis and evaluation that you will decide whether to accept the arguments, treat them with caution, or reject them. Your own argument can also be based on a more direct assessment of evidence. For example, you might look at a study on the impact of health promotion on alcohol use in Finland. You may decide that the findings and conclusions are convincing and widely applicable, or you may judge that the study is too small to be significant, or that it is only relevant to a particular social context.

It is not sufficient to look at facts, ideas and issues in isolation. You must demonstrate a good understanding of how these things interrelate. For example, you might compare and contrast several studies on the causes of alcohol misuse to determine if their findings are similar. If they are, this could provide powerful evidence to support a particular argument. If there are differences, you should try to find possible reasons for the differences. Could it be down to the different methodologies used, or are there other variables (eg age, gender, social context) which need to be taken into account? How do these facts impact on your own position?

Nuance

Students sometimes lack confidence in expressing their viewpoint in case it is 'wrong'. But your viewpoint is as valid as anyone else's, so long as it is supported with reasoned argument and sound evidence. However, being confident in your stance does not mean being rigid or close-minded. In fact, your stance should be **nuanced**. This means acknowledging strengths, weaknesses and grey areas. It entails, for example, sometimes *qualifying* your arguments or introducing *caveats* ('health promotion is a good way of tackling alcohol misuse *but* only if there is a consistent message across partner institutions'), or taking account of small but important differences in perspective (studies might have similar findings but interpret them in slightly different ways; two scholars may broadly agree that there is currently a lack of training on alcohol issues for nurses who work in General Practice, but have different ideas on how this should be remedied). A nuanced stance shows that you have been circumspect in your investigation and that you have not rushed to judgement. You must also be sure to recognise any limitations with regard to your own evidence, arguments or conclusions, and to clarify your position regarding which issues can be said to be resolved, and which remain open to debate.

CROSS
REFERENCE

Chapter 2,
Coherent
texts and
arguments,
Developing
a coherent
argument and
expressing
criticality

Nuance is very important in nursing essays which involve an examination of professional ethics and values. These are obviously complex issues, and it is expected that this complexity will be reflected in your discussion.

Expressing stance

Stance is conveyed through the way you treat your content, and through the way you organise and express your ideas. There are particular language features associated with the expression of stance (Biber, 2006; Argent, 2017). This will be explored through the task below, and in Chapter 2, where the organisation and expression of argument is explored in further detail.

Task

Writing critically

How is stance conveyed in the typical examples of student writing below? (Consider, for example, how the writers signal their analysis, evaluation, reasoning, interpretations, feelings and attitude.)

A

Research into psychosis has often focused on the role of the family. In the 1950s (when 'schizophrenia' was the more widely adopted term), the focus appeared to be on the family's role in the *causation* of psychosis. Consider, for example, Lidz et al's notion of 'pathological' families (1965) and the 'double-bind' hypothesis of Bateson et al (1956).

Around the same time as these 'causal' hypotheses were being promoted, the anti-psychotic drugs were discovered. Drugs, by their very nature, are treatments designated for the individual, and this fact, coupled with the prevailing view of families as toxic agents led, unsurprisingly, to what could cynically be called the first family intervention strategy – that of excluding the family.

B

One important element of communication in nursing is *active listening*, whereby nurses fully concentrate on and reflect on what patients say (Jagger, 2015). According to Mobley (2005), active listening is an effective way of signalling empathy, as it conveys to an individual that they have the full attention of the person they are talking to. One aspect of active listening is verbal communication on the part of the listener, such as restating and summarising the speaker's message (Jagger, 2015). Another important element of active listening is non-verbal communication. It is widely held that words form only a minor percentage of communication (Hargie et al, 2004; Sherman, 1993), and that a large part of any message is conveyed through 'paralanguage', such as tone of voice and intonation, and body language, such as posture, eye contact, facial expressions, gestures and touch (Argyle, 1988). This fact impacts considerably on the active listener, who not only has to be aware of the message conveyed through their own non-verbal communication, but also of any non-verbal cues from the speaker: 'One sigh may be communicating a lifetime of emotions' (Freshwater, 2003, p 93).

Discussion: writing critically

In these texts, examples of reasoning include:

- discussion of cause and effect

  This fact, coupled with the prevailing view of families as toxic agents **led**, unsurprisingly, **to** what could cynically be called the first family intervention strategy – that of excluding the family.

  This fact **impacts** considerably **on** the active listener.

- giving reasons for something

  Active listening is an effective way of signalling empathy, **as** it conveys to an individual that they have the full attention of the person they are talking to.

- exemplifying and explaining (in the third example, the colon introduces an elaboration of the point)

Consider, **for example**, Lidz et al's notion of 'pathological' families (1965) and the 'double-bind' hypothesis of Bateson et al (1956).

This fact, coupled with the prevailing view of families as toxic agents led, unsurprisingly, to what could cynically be called the first family intervention strategy – **that of** excluding the family.

This fact impacts considerably on the active listener, who not only has to be aware of the message conveyed through their own non-verbal communication, but also of any non-verbal clues from the speaker: 'One sigh may be communicating a lifetime of emotions' (Freshwater, 2003: 93).

Analysis involves identifying relationships or patterns in the literature. This can be implicit in the organisation of ideas. In A, for example, notice how the writer, rather than just describing what each source says, uses his sources to exemplify a 'pattern' he/she has identified.

Research into psychosis has often focused on the role of the family. **In the 1950s** (when 'schizophrenia' was the more widely adopted term), **the focus appeared to be on the family's role in the** *causation* **of psychosis. Consider, for example**, Lidz et al's notion of 'pathological' families (1965) and the 'double-bind' hypothesis of Bateson et al (1956).

Much analysis of the literature involves this 'drawing together' of ideas, or, as in the example below (from a journal article), comparing and contrasting different studies or 'threads' in the literature (in this case what is happening now/what happened before), eg:

There have been **a number of studies** investigating women's views on the acceptability of the antenatal HIV test in pregnancy (Duffy et al., 1998; Simpson et al., 1998; Boyd et al., 1999). **However**, there are **limited** in-depth explorations of pregnant women's experiences. **Existing** literature tends to focus on issues such as mothering (Sandelowski and Barroso, 2003), decision-making (Kirshenbaum et al., 2004) and psychological impact (Nancy et al., 2004). **Previous** qualitative research has looked at pregnant women who were unaware of their HIV-positive status. Sanders, **for example**, presented powerful narratives of nine HIV-positive women's experiences of temporarily losing parental rights, and of how mothering positively impacted on their recovery.

(Adapted from Lingen-Stallard et al, 2016, p 32)

CROSS REFERENCE

Chapter 3, Referring to sources

The texts in the task also include:

- language which indicates the writer's interpretation of or relationship with information and ideas in the literature ('has often focused on'; 'it is widely held that'; 'according to', which suggests a neutral stance towards the idea; 'appeared to be' and 'could be called', which suggest a cautious stance);
- language which suggests the writer holds a certain attitude towards information or ideas, and wishes to evoke a particular response in the reader ('by their very nature', 'unsurprisingly', 'cynically', 'important', 'considerably', and, in the Lingen-Stallard extract above, 'powerful').

Stance can also be more subtly conveyed: the 'not only x but y' structure in Example B serves to indicate to the reader that the writer has identified 'y' (underlined) as the most important thing to focus on:

This fact impacts considerably on the active listener, who **not only** has to be aware of the message conveyed through their own non-verbal communication, **but also** of any <u>non-verbal cues</u> from the speaker

Top tips

Summarising your argument

One way of developing and testing your stance is to see if you can write a single-sentence statement which you think summarises your argument. You can return to this statement as you read and write, and adapt it if necessary to reflect your changing thought processes. You may find that the final form of your statement ultimately forms part of your conclusion.

Task

Summarising your argument

Which of these statements represent **valid arguments** for the essay titles given below (and 'unpacked' earlier in the chapter)?

A

Given the many factors that might influence the health of an individual, consider the question: 'Can nurses really influence the health of others?'

Statement 1

Nurses can influence the health of others to some extent, but certain other factors such as diet and socio-economic status tend to have a more significant impact.

Statement 2

It is not up to nurses to tell people what to do. Individuals are responsible for their own lives.

Statement 3

Nurses should do more to help people improve their health.

Statement 4

There are many factors which influence the health of an individual, but nurses are in a prime position to make the most significant impact on an individual's health.

B

'The core skill of nursing is the ability to communicate.' Using appropriate evidence, explore the arguments for and against this proposition.

Statement 1

Nurses need to improve their communication skills as communication is the core skill of nursing.

Statement 2

Communication is important but it is just one of many skills which are key to nursing, some others being clinical skills and critical thinking.

Statement 3

Nurses require a variety of skills in their work, but the ability to communicate is the most important.

Statement 4

Nurses need a range of skills, including clinical skills and communication skills.

Discussion: summarising your argument

- Regarding Essay A, statements 1 and 4 are both valid arguments, as they recognise the premise that there are many factors influencing an individual's health, while also reflecting the emphasis in the essay title on the particular role of nurses. They convey different points of view, or stances, on how influential that role is (ie they have different interpretations of the literature, which they will need to justify), but this is to be expected. Statements 2 and 3 are just rather rash personal opinions, only loosely connected to the essay task.
- Regarding Essay B, statements 2 and 3 relate directly to the essay task, reflecting its clear focus on communication skills, even though they disagree on the relative importance of communication skills in comparison with other skills. Statements 1 and 4 are superficially related to the essay task, but they do not reflect the coverage or balance required.

The importance of evidence

To write critically, you need to be objective and able to distinguish between what is fact and what is theory. The more factual evidence you can collect to support theories, the sounder the arguments you will be able to make. For example, we cannot be *absolutely* certain that smoking causes lung cancer or that HIV causes AIDS, but that is the way the bulk of the evidence currently points. You are entitled to have your own opinions, and you will not necessarily fail for disagreeing with current thinking (or, indeed, disagreeing with the views of your lecturers). However, you will almost certainly fail if you do not provide sufficient evidence (in the form of references) to back up your views.

The examples below contrast vague, overgeneralised or unsubstantiated statements with evidence-based claims.

Nurses **are** generally happy with their pay and conditions. ✗

A recent report (Department of Health, 2016) **suggests that** nurses are generally happy with their pay and conditions. ✓

It is a fact that women who smoke are more likely to get breast cancer. ✗

Recent evidence (eg Kelly, 2015) points to a larger risk of breast cancer among women who smoke. ✓

Research **has proved that** women are more likely to care for sick or elderly relatives than men. ✗

Research **indicates that** women are more likely to care for sick or elderly relatives than men (Green, 2008). ✓

You can provide balanced arguments by comparing and contrasting evidence from different sources.

There is little evidence to support a wholesale expansion of practice nursing in cost terms alone. Thomas (2014), **however**, argues that other factors, such as the fact that the presence of nurses in GP surgeries and health centres is extremely popular among patients, should be taken into account.

Despite government figures which suggest that social-care funding is at the highest level it has been since records began in the mid-1950s, Smith (2012) **maintains** that social care is grossly under-funded.

On the one hand, nurses are, on the whole, in better health than the general population (Johnson, 2009). **On the other hand**, there are a significant number of nurses who are overweight, smoke and do not participate in any form of exercise (Department of Health, 2008).

Remember that not all evidence is equal. Be prepared to acknowledge when evidence is absent, unclear, contradictory, or not relevant to the current context.

Top tips

Putting ideas 'in the dock'

Try to think of academic arguments as a court case. You are a member of the jury and, before you make up your mind, you must listen to both the 'defence' (the arguments for) and the 'prosecution' (the arguments against). Hopefully, you wouldn't convict someone of a crime before listening to both sides and seeing what evidence is presented, so why believe unconditionally what academics have to say?

Writing essays

A critical essay is an in-depth exploration of a topic written in a formal style. The starting point for an essay may be a question for you to answer or a proposition for you to evaluate. Compare:

How important is it for nurses to possess good communication skills?

'The core skill of nursing is the ability to communicate.' Using appropriate evidence, explore the arguments for and against this proposition.

CROSS REFERENCE

Chapter 4, Language in use, Academic style

Essays involve discussion of theories and concepts which are key to your development as a nurse, and they often provide an opportunity for you to apply these theories or concepts to a real-world nursing context.

Essay structure

Good essays have a structure to them – in simple terms, they have a **beginning**, a **middle** and an **end**. This resembles the narrative structure of novels and films, and in many ways, an essay is the 'story' of your investigation of a topic.

CROSS REFERENCE

Appendix 4, Academic levels at university; Chapter 2, Coherent texts and arguments, Writing essay introductions and conclusions

Introduction (the 'beginning')

The introduction 'sets the scene' of the essay, telling the reader what you are writing about and why it is important. In this section, you should explain how you propose to achieve your purpose in writing, ie how you will tackle the requirements of the essay title or question. You should provide some background information and outline the main concepts under discussion (providing clarifications and/or definitions if necessary). You should also include a brief outline which indicates the structure of the essay. The outline should reflect the actual ordering of information in the essay and relate directly to any headings and subheadings. This will help to make sure that you stick to the task in hand, and it will ultimately help the reader to navigate your essay. Aim to use approximately 20 to 25 per cent of your word limit for the introduction.

Main body of the text (the 'middle')

This part should form the bulk of your essay – as much as 60 to 70 per cent of your word count. It can be written as one large section, but the reader must be able to discern blocks of content relating to each subsection mentioned in your introductory outline (and smaller sections within this). You might find it useful to divide the text using appropriate subheadings. (Your department may have particular requirements with regard to this, so always check the assessment guidelines.) In the main body, you must meet the requirements of the essay title or question, according to the academic level you are expected to be at. So, for example, if you are asked to write a second-year (Level 5; Level 8 in Scotland) essay about the value of health promotion in tackling alcohol misuse (discussed earlier in this chapter), you will need to explore the arguments for and against health promotion in this area. As many points of view as you can obtain must be taken into account, even if you don't agree with them – you are aiming to be as objective as possible.

Summary and/or conclusion (the 'end')

Summaries and conclusions shouldn't be more than about 10 to 15 per cent of your word limit. A summary expresses the main points of your essay in one or two paragraphs. It is not always necessary to have one, but it can be especially useful in longer (3,500+ word) essays. A conclusion usually refers the reader back to the introduction, to show you have achieved your stated purpose. It draws together the main points discussed in the body of the essay, and reiterates your stance. A conclusion allows you to make some decisions about the topic under discussion. At Level 5, for example, you have three options when concluding (as discussed earlier in this chapter): (i) you can come down in favour of the arguments for the issue being discussed ('health promotion is a good way to tackle alcohol misuse'); (ii) you can come down in favour of the arguments against the issue ('health promotion is a waste of time'); or (iii) you can be a 'fence-sitter' and remain undecided in the face of conflicting evidence. All three options are equally acceptable, so long as your decision is backed up by appropriate evidence.

A **coherent** essay contains arguments which fit your position and lead naturally to your conclusion.

Reflective essays

A reflective essay, as the name suggests, is based on **reflection**. Reflection is the critical analysis of a situation or event, and of your own experience, perceptions, behaviour and thought processes. It can involve analysing situations and events that go well, or not so well. It is a way of making sense of your experience, and relating it to your wider studies and professional development, establishing meaningful connections between theory and practice. It is essential to the development of your knowledge, understanding and intellectual development. Reflection provides an opportunity to think deeply about your beliefs and attitudes, and to explore the values which underpin nursing practice.

Reflective practice, the process whereby you stop and think about what you are doing on a day-to-day basis, is central to nursing. It facilitates continuous learning in what is an ever-changing context.

Reflective essays revolve around an account of a particular event or experience in your practice, something that, on reflection, you view as a **learning experience**. This is known as reflection *on* action, ie looking back at something that has passed, as opposed to reflection *in* action, ie thinking about your current action (Schön, 1987) – though both are important in nursing practice. Reflective essays are usually based on **reflective models**. One of the most well known of these consists of three simple questions (Borton, 1970):

- What?
- So what?
- Now what?

Another widely used model is Gibbs' Reflective Cycle (see Figure 1.1):

CROSS REFERENCE

Studying for your Nursing Degree, Chapter 3, Becoming a member of your academic and professional community, The nursing community

CROSS REFERENCE

Studying for your Nursing Degree, Chapter 4, Critical thinking, Critical thinking in clinical practice

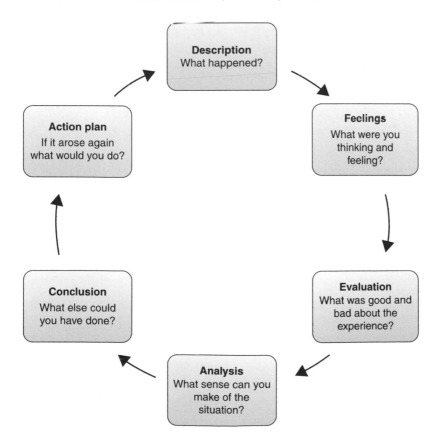

Figure 1.1: Gibbs' Reflective Cycle (adapted from Gibbs, 1988, p 50)

These reflective models provide a natural structure for a reflective essay.

- They first focus your thoughts on **what happened**, how you perceived an event or experience, and how you felt about it (Borton's 'What?'; Gibbs' 'description' and 'feelings'). This event or experience is commonly known as a **critical incident**, ie something that impacts on you in a significant way, either positively or negatively. Obvious critical incidents in life include the death of a loved one or the birth of your first child, but they can also be something more mundane (though still important in terms of your personal and professional development), like a difficult encounter with a colleague or patient.

- The models then focus on the **meaning** of the critical incident (Borton's 'So what?; Gibbs' 'evaluation' and 'analysis'). Your critical analysis and evaluation of your experience should be informed by the literature, which can help you make sense of the issues which arise. So if, for example, you are writing a reflective essay on the first time you nursed someone with a terminal illness, you would probably want to explore your anxieties about death, about any potential pain and discomfort the patient might feel, about dealing with distressed relatives, and so on. To do this, you might examine the literature on the feelings and experiences of nurses, and/or palliative care literature. Bear in mind, however, that you would be looking at the literature not just to describe nursing practices, but to compare and contrast your feelings and experiences with those of others, and to find ways of overcoming the anxieties you have.

- The final consideration covered by the models is **action**, ie how different courses of action might have played out, what you might do if a similar situation arose in the future (Borton's 'What now?'; Gibbs' 'conclusion' and 'action plan'). This comprises an assessment of the impact the experience has had on your understanding and future practice, detailing any insights you have gained, and any actions you need to take in order to enhance your personal development or professional practice.

You might find that you are provided with a template by your programme or module lecturers to help you reflect, based on the above models. Alternatively, you might find it helpful to create a template of your own, perhaps based on a reflective model you like.

Reflective essays are, like other essays, formal in style. However, check assessment guidelines for information on, for example, the use of tenses and personal pronouns. You will usually need to use a range of tenses, for example, the past tense to describe the incident, the present to discuss your current beliefs, and the future to report future planned action. It is also often necessary or natural to use personal pronouns in a reflective essay, eg:

> I noted that the patient's ankles were swollen.
>
> I reported the incident to the staff nurse.

However, where personal pronouns are rather 'chatty', and are easily replaced, it is better to avoid them, eg:

> I thought the patient was asleep. ✗
>
> The patient appeared to be asleep. ✓
>
> I know I need to find out more about this condition. ✗
>
> It is clear that I need to find out more about this condition. ✓

Top tips

Writing reflectively

1) Reflections are personal, but try to put some distance between you and the critical incident so that you can evaluate it as objectively as possible. Your objectivity should be reflected in your tone, which should be calm, restrained, and factual, eg 'the nurse confronted the patient and this made the other staff uneasy' rather than 'the nurse went for the patient making everyone not want to be there'.

2) Don't make assumptions and be cautious in your assessments. It is difficult to judge a situation when you have limited information. You cannot usually be sure why someone is behaving in a particular way, but you can speculate, eg 'she *seemed* anxious, *perhaps* because she was uncomfortable with the situation'.

3) Do not confuse your perception with fact, eg 'she *came across as* a bully' rather than 'she *is* a bully'; 'he *appeared to have* dementia' rather than 'he *clearly had* dementia'.

4) Be respectful in the way you refer to people, eg 'an *elderly* woman' rather than 'an *old* woman'; 'a young adult with a suspected eating disorder' rather than 'an anorexic girl'.

5) Anonymise participants. This can be done by using official titles ('the senior nurse') or pseudonyms.

Task

Reflective essays

Which section of a reflective essay do you think the following extracts come from? What tells you this? Can you relate them to the reflective models discussed above?

A

Joseph (a pseudonym), a 62-year-old patient with end-stage lung cancer, was admitted for palliative care and pain relief to the ward I was on placement with. His relatives had a number of concerns regarding his condition and treatment. They were clearly very distressed.

B

Seeing Joseph in obvious pain, and his family in distress, made me worry about my own emotions, whether I might get visibly upset or say the 'wrong' thing to the family. The times when I felt less in control of my own emotions were when I witnessed his daughter and teenage grandson, who were very close to him, getting really upset because of Joseph having difficulty breathing. I felt unsure of how to manage my emotions so that I could maintain a balance between natural empathy and professionalism.

C

I discussed things with my mentor, who advised me that it was important to be open, honest and compassionate with Joseph and his family. She said communication skills were absolutely essential in these circumstances, and that while ensuring Joseph was made as physically comfortable as possible, I should also ask everyone if they were OK, if they needed anything, if they wanted to ask questions, and so on. While, she said, it was natural to be upset when seeing others distressed, she also said most student nurses soon learnt how to balance their emotions so that they came across as both compassionate and professional. She offered me the opportunity to talk to her on a regular basis if I was worried I was going to be upset.

D

Following my mentor's advice, I found the family were extremely grateful for the attention I gave them, as well as Joseph. I also found it was easier to handle my emotions than I first thought. The NMC Code (2015) states that nurses should 'share with people, their families and their carers, as far as the law allows, the information they want or need to know about their health, care and ongoing treatment sensitively and in a way they can understand'. I now fully understand why this part of the Code is so important in practice. In future, I will endeavour to be approachable and ensure that patients and their loved ones are given appropriate information. Since the Code also says nurses should 'make sure that any information or advice given is evidence-based', I have arranged some time with a Marie Curie nurse and will do some reading around the topic.

Writing short reflections for journals or portfolios

You will usually be required to submit short written reflections (approximately 300–1,000 words) for assessment as part of your nursing degree (distinct from the 'reflective essay' discussed previously in this chapter). These written reflections are also key to **professional portfolio** development for nursing students and practitioners alike, so writing in this way is a skill you will need to take with you when qualified. Reflective writing sometimes permeates whole course units, or even entire programmes of study, via a **reflective diary** (also known as a **reflective journal** or **reflective log**) that requires regular entries.

As with a reflective essay, a mixture of tenses is used as you move between past, present and future. However, in contrast to an essay, the writing style used in reflective accounts in journals or for portfolios can be relatively conversational, and the first person pronoun ('I') is almost always used.

Task

Reflective writing

1) Look at the piece of reflective writing below. What do you notice about the following?
   - the style of writing;
   - the use of tenses;
   - the relation to the reflective models (Borton, Gibbs) discussed in the previous section.

On an older people's ward, I went to talk to a man because he looked like he was upset. I asked him his name but he just snapped and told me to get lost and mind my own business. He was the same when his wife came in. It upset me a bit but I wondered if everything was OK with him so I asked my mentor. She explained that they thought he may have dementia and that this sort of behaviour was common in people with undiagnosed dementia and that I shouldn't take anything personally. I did some reading on dementia after the shift and it made me understand why he might be behaving in the way he was. I will talk to the mentor tomorrow to see if she has any tips or advice on how I might be able to communicate with him better.

2) Compare the two reflections, A and B, below. What are the main differences? Which one is not acceptable and why?

A

I had real difficulties on Ward A2 at Manchester East Hospital because Sr Johnson was a bully. She treated the daughter of Mrs Kenton, a 75-year-old lady with dementia, appallingly, asking her to leave on several occasions. Michael and Katie, the 2nd and 3rd years who were on duty with me, agreed that she was a bully, but Michael said there's usually a reason why people are bullies, so perhaps Sr Johnson was having a bad time. He thought her marriage was breaking up.

I contacted Sharon, the Practice Education Facilitator. She then told Sr Johnson, which really scared me and Michael and Katie as I thought we'd all be in trouble. We weren't, and Sr Johnson was actually quite nice, apologising to us.

This whole placement has made me think twice about wanting to carry on nursing.

B

I had real difficulties on my last placement (an older people's ward) because one of the senior members of nursing staff came across as a bully. There was a particular incident with the daughter of a 75-year-old lady with dementia that really upset me. Two other students who were on duty with me also thought that the senior member of staff was 'difficult'.

I contacted the Practice Education Facilitator (PEF) for the ward and my academic adviser at uni and explained how we all felt. The PEF went and spoke to the senior member of staff in confidence, and she asked if she might meet us with the PEF. The PEF and my academic adviser reassured us we wouldn't be in trouble, and although the meeting was quite scary for us students, they were right. The senior member of staff apologised profusely, saying both her parents had recently been diagnosed with dementia and she was very stressed. She also explained that she'd been having difficulties with the 75-year-old lady's daughter, because the daughter had been subtly threatening and making racist comments to an Asian family on the ward. She said she was sorry that she came across as abrupt, and she thanked us for bringing the issue to her attention. (She also told us that when the PEF had initially raised the matter with her she was shocked that she had come across that way.)

This episode made me realise that I shouldn't judge people immediately and that it's always best to bring concerns to the attention of the appropriate people. I finished the placement some six weeks later thinking it was actually a very good placement for students and that I shouldn't be scared to raise concerns.

Discussion: reflective writing

1) The reflection mostly follows the reflective models (Borton, 1970; Gibbs, 1988) discussed earlier in the chapter: the writer describes the critical incident, and her feelings about it, and there is some analysis of the wider issue, ie the reasons behind the incident; she also describes the action she has taken to help understand the illness better, and indicated future action, ie seeking advice from her mentor. The style is relatively conversational, there are informal expressions ('get lost', 'mind my own business', 'upset me a bit'), and the first person ('I') is used throughout. However, it is not overly chatty or in any way inappropriate – in fact, it is **restrained** and **thoughtful** ('upset me *a bit*', 'I *might*'). The **critical incident** is related **calmly** and **factually**. It is clear that the student has understood the **value of reflection** and the nature of the **learning process**. The 'narrative' is related in the past tense ('she treated', 'I contacted'), present tense is used for facts ('is behaving'), and future is used for planned action ('I will talk').

2) Reflection A describes a critical incident, but it is related in a rather clumsy, judgemental fashion, and where there should be analysis, there is only really gossip and speculation. The student does not seem to have learned anything useful from the incident, and her conclusion on future action does not seem very measured, or to really be a logical consequence of what has happened. Reflection A is also clearly problematic in terms of confidentiality because it names the clinical area, a specific member of staff, a patient, and a patient's relative, as well as some fellow students and the Practice Education Facilitator (PEF).

   Reflection B is much better. The language used to relate the critical incident is much more **cautious** and **restrained**: 'came across as a bully' rather than 'was a bully'; the choice of the rather diplomatic word 'difficult' and the accompanying use of quotation marks. The analysis of the incident is **calm** and **factual**, and sensible future action has been identified – notice the use of the present tense here, as the actions refer to general behaviour ('I shouldn't'; 'it's always best to') rather than a particular future plan. The participants are not identifiable. They are referred to in a general sense ('one of the senior members of staff', 'a 75-year-old lady with dementia', etc).

Writing in exams

Examinations test your ability to recall information and write under pressure. However, as with any written assignment, you should read the question or task carefully and highlight key words. You can use the exam booklet to jot down basic ideas and outlines, as long as you cross out any rough work before handing it in. In exams, you do not have a lot of time to spend thinking about organisation, expression or presentation, and examiners will take this into account. Nonetheless, whatever you can do to make the examiner's life easier will count in your favour – remember, your exam script may come from the middle of a pile of 200 or more!

Top tips

Exam strategies

- In a long answer, stick to one point per paragraph and leave a line between paragraphs. This will make your exam script easier to read.
- Make your handwriting as clear as possible – you can get no credit for ideas if no one can read them.
- Make it clear which question you are answering.

Assessment task

Answering exam questions

Look at the exam question below and the students' answers. Have they answered the question well? Why/why not?

'Care that is not compassionate is not care'. Discuss.

Answer A

Proficient nursing requires three key things: (1) technical ability in clinical skills (the ability to carry out nursing procedures safely and competently); (2) intellectual ability (eg critical thinking and problem-solving skills); and (3) appropriate attitudes and values. A nurse may have the technical ability to carry out specific nursing procedures safely and competently; she may also be aware of the underpinning evidence base for those procedures. However, to be truly effective, care must also be compassionate. This involves, for example, being sensitive to the patient's needs and being non-judgemental. A lack of compassion often results in a breakdown of care, as the Francis Report (2013) found. In this case, the lack of compassion in nursing care was not seen as necessarily down to 'bad' nursing and support staff; rather, it emerged from an erosion in values by a prevailing culture driven by targets and finance. Thus, leadership clearly has a role to play in facilitating and maintaining compassionate care.

Answer B

Care has to be compassionate because the Chief Nurse said so in her 6Cs initiative. The 6Cs stand for care, compassion, competence, communication, courage and commitment. The Francis Report said nurses were not compassionate; therefore we have to do something about it. The best way of being compassionate is to read the notes that we get on compassionate care at uni. I always think of the 6Cs when I am in practice and I know my patients get compassionate care from me because my mentor wrote 'compassionate care given' in a patient I looked after's notes. Nurses who are not compassionate should be removed from the NMC Register.

Discussion: answering exam questions

- Answer A situates the discussion question in a clear context and provides an independent point of view, supported by examples, and an appraisal of wider implications.
- Answer B does not answer the question. It states facts without offering any analysis. Many statements are unsubstantiated or purely anecdotal. It meanders from point to point, and the style is rather informal and chatty.

Writing dissertations

A dissertation is a long evidence-based or research-focused essay, usually between 10,000 and 20,000 words. It shares many of the requirements discussed in relation to critical essays, such as having a clear purpose and strategy, a defined target reader, a conventional structure, and a well-developed stance and argument. An **evidence-based** nursing dissertation could involve conducting your own review of the evidence surrounding a particular nursing practice, treatment or care approach. A **research-focused** dissertation could involve investigation of a current 'knowledge gap' or 'problem' in the field of nursing. However, because of the strict ethics associated with conducting research, undergraduate nursing students tend not to do research-focussed dissertations (though this is an expectation of most postgraduate dissertations).

Before you start your dissertation, you will have to write a **proposal** outlining your chosen line of enquiry. You will need to make it clear that the dissertation is feasible, and that you have the knowledge and skills to carry it out. You will also need to outline any potential challenges or problems you foresee. With research dissertations, you will need to complete the ethics form prescribed by your university. Finally, you will need to include an initial bibliography, ie sources that you think will be of use to you.

Like all essays, dissertations must have a 'beginning', a 'middle' and an 'end'. An **introduction** provides background information on the topic under review, or the gap or problem under investigation. The introduction also presents the rationale for your current review or investigation, and outlines how you intend to go about your study. A **conclusion** serves to draw everything together with a summary of the main argument and its implications for nursing practice.

The 'middle' part of a dissertation is founded on an extensive **literature review**, presenting an analysis and evaluation of current scholarship on the topic, and detailing key concepts, theories and arguments.

Research-focused dissertations may adopt the **IMRAD** structure found in many scientific journal articles:

- Introduction;
- Method;
- Results;
- Discussion.

With this structure, the introduction and literature review comprise a single section, though they are sometimes separated. Your **methodology** describes the type of study you are conducting (quantitative, qualitative, mixed methods), and your methods of data collection and analysis (eg a survey, statistical analysis). It also covers any ethical considerations. The **results** section details the findings of your study; tables and figures are often useful tools in this section. The **discussion** section is where you interpret your findings and discuss their meaning and significance. This will involve relating what you have found out to current knowledge in the field, and highlighting any new insights or understanding. Sometimes in nursing, hypothetical research is proposed, in which case only the methodology section is included. The 'discussion' section then might be around the potential pitfalls in carrying out the research.

Dissertations also have an **abstract**, which comprises a short summary of the whole dissertation, and a list of **references**.

CROSS REFERENCE

Studying for your Nursing Degree, Chapter 3, Becoming a member of your academic and professional community, Academic principles, pursuits and practices, Teaching, research and knowledge

Summary

This chapter has introduced the topic of academic writing. It has explored the context of academic writing at university, and provided guidance on how to approach academic writing tasks in your nursing degree. It has explored some of the general principles of academic writing, the writing process, and important features of typical text types in nursing. It has also highlighted the centrality of criticality in writing, something which will be expanded on in subsequent chapters.

CROSS REFERENCE

Studying for your Nursing Degree, Chapter 3, Becoming a member of your academic and professional community, Advanced skills, Research reports

Sources of example texts

Lingen-Stallard, A, Furber, C and Lavender, T (2016) Testing HIV Positive in Pregnancy: A Phenomenological Study of Women's Experiences. *Midwifery*, 35, 31–38.

References

Academic Phrasebank. Available at: www.phrasebank.manchester.ac.uk (accessed 15 February 2017).

Argent, S (2017) The Language of Critical Thinking [online]. Available at: www.baleap.org/event/eap-northcritical-thinking (accessed 27 February 2017).

Biber, D (2006) Stance in Spoken and Written University Registers. *Journal of English for Academic Purposes*, 5(2), 97–116.

Borton, T (1970) *Reach, Touch and Teach: Student Concerns and Process Education.* London: Hutchinson.

Gibbs, G (1988) *Learning by Doing: A Guide to Teaching and Learning Methods.* Oxford: Further Education Unit, Oxford Polytechnic.

Schön, D (1987) *Educating the Reflective Practitioner: Towards a New Design for Teaching and Learning in the Professions.* San Francisco: Jossey-Bass.

Swales, J (1990) *Genre Analysis.* Cambridge: Cambridge University Press.

Swales, J and Feak, C (2012) *Academic Writing for Graduate Students: Essential Tasks and Skills.* 3rd ed. Michigan: Michigan ELT.

Woodford, P (1967) Sounder Thinking Through Clearer Writing. *Science,* 156(3776), 743–45.

Chapter 2
Coherent texts and arguments

Reflection

1) What do you think it means to write 'coherently'? How do you think this can be achieved?

2) What do you understand by 'a coherent argument'? How is a coherent argument constructed?

3) How do you go about planning a piece of written work? How much time do you spend on this?

4) How do you go about editing a piece of written work? How much time do you spend on this?

If a text is **coherent**, it **makes sense to the reader**. In this chapter, you will analyse a range of academic nursing texts to help you understand how coherence is achieved. Alongside this, you will develop effective planning, writing and editing strategies so that you are able to produce coherent texts and arguments of your own.

Planning for coherence

Planning is the process of selecting and organising information and ideas in order to respond to an assignment task effectively. The planning process should start with an examination of the wording of the task or question. This involves analysing, or 'unpacking', it so that you can be sure about what the lecturer assessing your work is expecting you to do.

When you are sure you understand what you are being asked to do, you should start to draft a plan or 'outline'.

An outline is much more than a mere list of topics; there should be a clear **organising principle**, both for the text as a whole, and for individual sections of the text. This might involve presenting items chronologically, or in order of importance; it often involves starting with general information and moving on to more specific information. Your outline should indicate how individual items relate to the main topic and to each other, ie how they are governed by your main organising principle.

Below are some examples of common organisational frameworks (for a piece of writing, or for sections of a piece of writing) which can help you to organise information and ideas (Jordon, 2001):

- **classification**, ie the division of something into groups, classes, categories etc, usually according to specific criteria;
- **comparison and contrast**, ie an examination of similarities and differences;

CROSS REFERENCE

Chapter 1, Academic writing: text, process and criticality, Analysing a writing assignment

CROSS REFERENCE

General and specific information

- **cause and effect**, ie how one thing influences another; what results from certain situations or actions;
- **problem-solution**, ie the description and analysis of a problem, and the evaluation of possible solutions to that problem.

Other common elements of academic texts include **description**, **narrative**, **definition of key terms**, and **exemplification**. These different elements may overlap: there is likely to be discussion of the causes and effects of a problem; classification may well require discussion of similarities and differences; description, definition of key terms, and exemplification are integral to many organisational frameworks.

Task

Organisational frameworks

 1) What organisational principles are being employed in the essay plans below?

A

<u>Factors that might influence an individual's health</u>

- diet, eg obesity, diabetes
- environment, eg access to clean water
- lifestyle, eg smoking
- socio-economic status, eg poor housing, damp etc
- cultural factors, eg travellers' cultural beliefs – eg on what is 'pure/impure' – informs attitudes on vaccinations (Van Cleemput et al, 2007)
- health practitioners, eg GPs, nurses, midwives

B

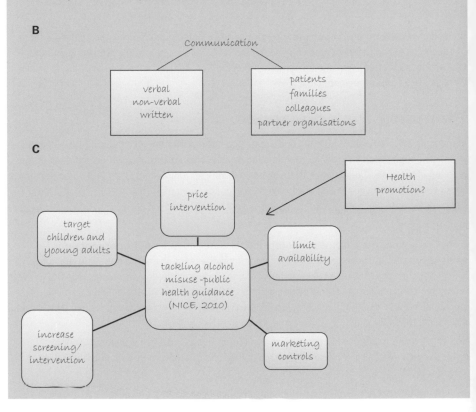

D

Women's experience of being HIV in pregnancy (Lingen-Stallard et al, 2016)

- shock and disbelief
- anger and turmoil
- acceptance and resilience

E

- Mature student nurses – valuable life experience; particularly drawn to difficult to recruit areas such as mental health (RCN, www.rcn.org.uk/news-and-events/news/mature-students-decide-against-nursing, 2017)
- Significant drop in applications from over 25s (RCN) – loss of bursaries/introduction of fees?
- Targeted recruitment drive?

F

Should young people be given antidepressants? (Kendal and Pryjmachuk 2011)

Cotgrove, 2007	Timini, 2007
- cites studies that show benefits (NCCMH, 2005; Whittington et al, 2004) - claims alternative therapies such as CBT, interpersonal therapy and family therapy have limited effect	- questions evidence - believes most childhood distress is self-limiting and does not require extensive intervention - believes marketing spin has taken precedence over scientific accuracy - claims link between antidepressants and suicide

2) Which of the sections below do you think are relevant to the essay provided? How could the relevant sections be effectively organised?

A

Given the many factors that might influence the health of an individual, consider the question: 'Can nurses really influence the health of others?'

Introduction/background – refer to title

- Factors influencing an individual's health (diet, environment, lifestyle, socio-economic status, cultural factors)
- Definition of nurse
- Definition of health
- Concept of 'empowerment'
- Contextualise to my field of nursing
- Extent to which nurses can influence
- Compare with influence of other health professionals, eg doctors

Conclusion – can have an impact, but other factors (eg clean water, cessation of smoking) have more – potential of nurses to influence these things?

B

'The core skill of nursing is the ability to communicate.' Using appropriate evidence, explore the arguments for and against this proposition.

Introduction/background – claimed that communication is the core skill of nursing

- Definition of communication
- Definition of proposition

- Relative importance of (other) different core skills (NMC): leadership, intellectual skills, admin skills, clinical skills – less important than communication?
- All nurses should learn a foreign language
- Problems caused by breakdown in communication (eg Francis report)
- Different types of communication: verbal, written, non-verbal
- How communication impacts on other aspects of nursing – thus more important?
- Different forms of communication: patients, families, colleagues, partner organisations
- Communication is more of a concern for managers than nurses

Conclusion – nurses need a range of skills but communication is integral to all, and very difficult to be a good nurse without good communication skills, even if competent in 'technical' skills

Editing and redrafting for coherence

Editing is a process whereby a writer makes changes to the content, organisation and expression of a text in order to improve it. The writing and editing process is also referred to as 'drafting' and 'redrafting', with writers producing different 'drafts' of a text. (Lecturers may sometimes ask you to submit 'a first draft' – though this does not mean that it should be unedited! It is probably best to think of this as 'an early draft'.)

The truth about writing!

If you lack experience in academic writing, it can sometimes feel as if you are a 'novice', 'outside', looking 'in' on the world of 'expert' writers (academics and experienced student writers), where everyone gets everything right first time. But this is far from the truth! In fact, you are a member of a diverse **writing community**, and members from all levels of this community, including experienced writers, usually have to work very hard to produce text which is clear and coherent. In order to make sure their writing makes sense to the reader, it is usually necessary for most writers to read and edit their text frequently at all stages of the writing process. It is tempting to believe that you will be able to get away with less editing as you become more experienced in writing, but in fact, research suggests that the more experienced a writer becomes, the more they edit and redraft (Benson and Heidish, 1995). If experienced academics see the value and necessity of the editing and redrafting process, then it seems advisable that you, as a developing academic writer, should follow their example.

Putting yourself in the reader's shoes

If you do not read your own text, you cannot imagine the reader's experience as they navigate the text. You should read your text frequently, *putting yourself in the reader's shoes*. As you read, ask yourself the following questions:

- Would this make sense to someone else?
- Are points and ideas organised according to clear principles?
- Are they in a logical order?
- Are the links between them explicit?
- Is there anything which is vague or ambiguous?
- Does the text *flow*?

When reading and editing, your focus should be on **meaning**; at a later stage, you will need to proofread your text in order to correct surface errors in grammar and punctuation, but this should not be the focus while you are still at the stage of making decisions about content and organisation. You also need to leave time at the end of the writing process to read through the text several times. Again, you should first focus on meaning (before proofreading). Being able to do this also requires good time management: you can't do it if you finish the essay ten minutes before the deadline!

CROSS
REFERENCE

Chapter 5,
Preparing
your work for
submission

Task

Editing and redrafting for coherence

Look at the following drafts. Text A is accurate and academic in style, but the lecturer reading it found it a little hard to follow, as indicated by the comments. What changes has the writer made in B in order to make the text more coherent for the reader?

What kind of changes?

A

Bit vague

Burrells et al (2015) argue that nurses are instrumental in helping patients make <u>changes</u> which could help them improve their long-term health prospects <u>because of diabetes</u>. <u>It</u> found that extension of the nursing role would not compromise quality of care or outcomes for patients. However, if nurses were to take on a greater share of patient care in general practice, this would have workforce implications.

What?

Not obvious you were discussing nurses in <u>general practice</u> up to this point

B

Burrells et al (2015) argue that general practice nurses are instrumental in helping diabetes patients make behavioural changes which could help them improve their long-term health prospects. In their study of nursing consultations and control of diabetes in GP surgeries, Burrells et al found no evidence to suggest that extension of the nursing role would in any way compromise quality of care or outcomes for these patients. However, if nurses were to take on a greater share of diabetes patient care in general practice, this would have workforce implications.

Discussion: editing and redrafting for coherence

Text B is clearer, as it is far more **explicit**.

CROSS
REFERENCE

Cohesion and
paragraph
structure,
Referring
back in
the text,
Repetition,
variation and
pronoun use

- It reminds the reader that the topic is *diabetes care* rather than just *care* in general by repeating the word 'diabetes' at several key points.
- The phrase 'behavioural changes' in Text B is much clearer than the rather vague 'changes'.
- Text B is explicit about the study being referred to, and the fact that it is focused on *general practice* rather than hospitals or home care. In Text A, the reader only realises that general practice is the focus right at the end of the text.
- In Text A, the reader is having to guess what 'it' refers to. It is important to be very sure that the reader can trace a pronoun like 'it' or 'they' back to the thing it refers to. This will be discussed later in this chapter.

Writing essay introductions and conclusions

A coherent essay makes things clear for the reader right from the start with a clear **introduction**. The introduction should tell the reader:

- Your purpose in writing. You should refer directly to the essay title or question.
- Some general background information, including the main concepts under discussion, clarifications, definitions etc.
- How you will address the topic in order to achieve your purpose and satisfy the needs and expectations of the reader. You should include a brief overview of what will be included in the essay in order to achieve the stated purpose. The items listed in this overview should reflect the order in which you present them in the essay (and refer to exact subheadings if you have them).

Below is an example introduction for one of the essays referred to earlier in the chapter:

'The core skill of nursing is the ability to communicate.' Using appropriate evidence, explore the arguments for and against this proposition.

> It has been claimed that the core skill of nursing is communication (Brain, 2014). It is abundantly clear that communication is important in nursing practice. Nurses are required to speak to patients, families and colleagues every day. They must also provide written communications, in the form of patient records, for example. However, it could be argued that clinical skills, intellectual skills, and even general administrative capacity are equally, if not more, important. **The aim of this essay is** to examine the extent to which communication can be considered to be the *core* nursing skill. **It will begin by** examining what is meant by the term 'communication' in nursing. **It will then** outline what are generally considered to be the core skills required by nurses, with reference to the NMC Code (2015). **It will go on** to examine the impact of communication skills on a range of nursing activities, and assess the role that poor communication has played in a number of documented 'failures' in nursing.

CROSS
REFERENCE

Linking ideas

Note the key phrases (in **bold**) used to indicate each section of the essay. Notice also the form of the verb that follows these phrases (the aim is *to do*; begin by *doing*; go on *to do*). These types of phrases, used to guide the reader through a text, are known as **signposts** (discussed later in the chapter). These signposts can be adapted to most essays, and they are a useful tool for ensuring that you have a clear structure. Common verbs for describing what a writer *does* in essays are:

- outline;
- describe;
- identify;
- examine;
- look into;
- analyse;
- evaluate;
- explore.

CROSS
REFERENCE

Appendix 3,
Key phrases in
assignments

These terms are not interchangeable: for example, they can express whether you intend to simply present or describe something, or whether you aim to go deeper. The terms you use should relate to the key terms used in the essay title or question.

Longer essays may have an introduction which provides quite an extended account of the essay context. An example can be seen later in this chapter.

CROSS
REFERENCE

Developing
a coherent
argument and
expressing
criticality

A **conclusion** is the part of the essay where you draw everything together. It usually contains the following:

- a reference to what was said in the introduction to show that you have achieved your stated purpose;
- a summary of your argument, drawing together the main points discussed in the body of the essay;
- a statement on where you stand on the topic you've discussed, and the significance of this;
- some practical recommendations and/or implications for nursing practice.

Below is an example of a conclusion for the same essay.

> In conclusion, good communication skills lie at the heart of all areas of nursing practice, and can thus be considered to be at least as important as the clinical and intellectual skills that a nurse must be proficient in. It is therefore important that communication skills are developed and assessed as part of nurse education. However, nurses do not function in isolation. As discussion of a number of reported nursing 'failures' in this essay has shown, a breakdown in communication between management and nurses can result in or contribute to poor patient care. Thus, it is clear that effective communication is something which should be prioritised at all levels of healthcare.

Cohesion and paragraph structure

A text is made up of paragraphs. For a text to be clear and coherent, each paragraph must have a clear focus and structure. Good paragraphs usually have the following structural characteristics:

- they deal with a single unified point and do not digress from this;
- they often introduce this point in the first sentence;
- they usually move from general to specific information and ideas;
- they order and connect ideas in a logical manner.

In order for a paragraph to develop clearly, the points or ideas it contains should be linked in *meaningful* ways. This meaningful linking is known as 'cohesion' (Halliday and Hassan, 1976), and it is achieved through organisation, grammar and word choice, aspects of which will be discussed in this section. (Note that the extracts in the following task will be referred to throughout this chapter.)

Task

Cohesion and paragraph structure

Read the paragraphs below.

1) Do you find them easy to read?

2) The paragraphs demonstrate some of the typical features of paragraph development and cohesion in English. Can you identify any aspects of organisation, grammar or word choice which make your life easier as a reader?

Extract A: An extract from a typical student essay

One important element of communication in nursing is *active listening*, whereby nurses fully concentrate on and reflect on what patients say (Jagger, 2015). According to Mobley (2005), active listening is an effective way of signalling empathy, as it conveys to an individual that they have the full attention of the person they are talking to. One aspect of active listening is verbal communication on the part of the listener, such as restating and summarising the speaker's message (Jagger, 2015). Another important element of active listening is non-verbal communication. It is widely held that words form only a minor percentage of communication (Hargie et al, 2004; Sherman, 1993), and that a large part of any message is conveyed through 'paralanguage', such as tone of voice and intonation, and body language, such as posture, eye contact, facial expressions, gestures and touch (Argyle, 1988). This fact impacts considerably on the active listener, who not only has to be aware of the message conveyed through their own non-verbal communication, but also of any non-verbal clues from the speaker: 'One sigh may be communicating a lifetime of emotions' (Freshwater, 2003, p 93).

Extract B: An extract from a nursing textbook (Tierney et al, 2015, p 345)

The assessment of a person's capacity to give or withhold consent is considered in relation to a specific decision. While the individual may not have capacity to make some decisions, they may still retain capacity for other decisions. For example, a patient may not have capacity to make a decision regarding a surgical procedure but could retain capacity to consent (or not) to having their clinical observations (e.g. blood pressure) checked.

Extract C: An extract from a nursing textbook (Pryjmachuk, 2011, p 36)

As far as individual nursing practice is concerned, mental health nurses more often than not adopt the perspective(s) that most appeal to them. However, given the current emphasis on evidence-based practice, it is important that we do not let ideological dogma alone dominate our practice. Though there are some practitioners who rigidly adhere to one or other of the theoretical frameworks, these are the exception rather than the rule. Most skilled practitioners take an eclectic approach: they have an awareness of the strengths and weaknesses of the various perspectives and models, and they use their professional judgement to select a treatment approach most suitable for a given set of circumstances.

> **Extract D: An (adapted) extract from the recommendations section of a research article (Lingen-Stallard et al, 2016, p 37)**
>
> Midwives should be better trained to support women who are diagnosed with HIV. This should include appropriate communication of results, offering individualised support, maintaining confidentiality and providing accurate information on the impact of an HIV positive test. The latter point is particularly important, as some participants automatically believed they had AIDS and that death would be imminent. Women need explicit information telling them the benefits of medication and crucially, that the transmission rate in children born to women with an HIV infection diagnosed prior to childbirth is under 1% (Tookey, 2013). Midwives should provide information on support groups following HIV infection and repeat this information throughout pregnancy and post birth. In addition to training midwives, support staff (eg receptionists) should also be trained to ensure that women's status remains confidential and stigmatisation does not occur. Midwives should recognise the potential consequences to women of revealing their status to their partners and should not feel pressurised to disclose their results.

General and specific information

As shown in Table 2.1, all the example paragraphs above move from **general** statements to more **specific** information, which is typical of English paragraph structure. General statements at the start of a paragraph often serve to establish the topic of the whole paragraph: these are sometimes called **topic sentences** or **umbrella statements**. As these examples show, specific information can include definitions, explanations, analysis, evidence, evaluation, and exemplification, but this varies depending on the purpose of the writer.

Table 2.1: General and specific content

EXAMPLE TEXT	GENERAL TOPIC	SPECIFIC DETAILS
A	Introduction to and definition of a key concept/term	Relevance, significance, analysis, evidence
B	General statement/claim	Explanation, exemplification
C	General statement/claim	Analysis, evaluation
D	Recommendation	Expansion, exemplification, focus on and exemplification of two points (information and confidentiality), evidence

Task

General and specific information

Identify and describe the general and specific information in the paragraph below.

> Managing the delivery of health and social care in the UK involves collaborating with a variety of complex organisations and professionals within a diverse workforce. Nowadays, healthcare staff are constantly under pressure to improve services often when resources are stretched. In certain circumstances this can result in a communication breakdown or poor provision of care which leads to frustration, particularly when this involves patients and relatives who may be anxious and upset, distressed or angry. Therefore it is somewhat inevitable that you will encounter difficult situations at some stage in your career.
>
> (Burns, 2015, p 218)

Old and new information

To respond to an academic assignment, it is necessary to provide the reader with a lot of information. However, it is also necessary to let the reader know how each new piece of information fits in with what has already been said. The example extracts above demonstrate one typical way of doing this in English: they frequently refer back to **'old'** information given in the previous sentence, or earlier in the text, before supplying **'new'** information. It is a way of staying on topic, linking ideas together, and focusing the reader on the new information. This feature is highlighted below: Extract A repeatedly refers to the main theme of the text (introduced in the first sentence), adding new information each time; The last sentence in A and the second and third sentences in D refer back to the theme of the previous sentence.

Theme

One important element of communication in nursing is **active listening**, whereby nurses fully concentrate on and reflect on what patients say (Jagger, 2015). According to Mobley (2005), **active listening** is an effective way of signalling empathy, as it conveys to an individual that they have the full attention of the person they are talking to. One aspect of **active listening** is verbal communication on the part of the listener, such as restating and summarising the speaker's message (Jagger, 2015). Another important element of **active listening** is non-verbal communication. It is widely held that words form only a minor percentage of communication (Hargie et al, 2004; Sherman, 1993), and that a large part of any message is conveyed through 'paralanguage', such as tone of voice and intonation, and body language, such as posture, eye contact, facial expressions, gestures and touch (Argyle, 1988). **This fact** impacts considerably on the **active listener**, who not only has to be aware of the message conveyed through their own non-verbal communication, but also of any non-verbal clues from the speaker: 'One sigh may be communicating a lifetime of emotions' (Freshwater, 2003, p 93).

Midwives should be better trained to support women who are diagnosed with HIV. **This** should include appropriate communication of results, offering individualised support, maintaining confidentiality and providing accurate information on the impact of an HIV positive test. **The latter point** is particularly important, as some participants automatically believed they had AIDS and that death would be imminent.

Task

Old and new information

Find the parts of the text below which refer back to information given earlier in the text.

Patients and service users are being encouraged to take more control of their own care (Department of Health, 2009) and they have an important part to play in determining how services are designed, implemented and evaluated (The Kings Fund, 2012). By collaborating with service users and responding appropriately to their feedback, nurses can deliver more appropriate care and ensure that any concerns raised are dealt with quickly and appropriately (Coulter, 2012). This will usually involve collecting and using information provided by patients (e.g. patient satisfaction surveys or focus groups) in order to deliver the kind of services that patients want. Whichever approach is used, the key aim is to find out what patients really think about the services we provide and provide supporting evidence of this.

(Burns, 2015, p 228)

Referring back in the text: repetition, variation and pronoun use

Reference back to information earlier in the text can be achieved through repetition, as demonstrated in Extract A. Students are sometimes reluctant to repeat as they have been told that repetition will bore the reader or will indicate their lack of knowledge or vocabulary. The truth is that there is good and bad repetition: 'bad' repetition involves the inclusion of redundant information or words, or 'clumsy' reiteration of the same word in sequential sentences; 'good' repetition is a vital part of cohesion (Halliday and Hasan, 1976), and, used carefully, it greatly improves the lucidity of the text for the reader. In Extract A, repetition of the key term reminds the reader what the text is about, and enables them to understand how each new point relates to the central concept in question.

Another way of staying on topic is through 'chains' of related words through a text, for example, the use of words related to 'theory' in the following text.

> As far as individual nursing practice is concerned, mental health nurses more often than not adopt the **perspective(s)** that most appeal to them. However, given the current emphasis on evidence-based practice, it is important that we do not let **ideological** dogma alone dominate our practice. Though there are some practitioners who rigidly adhere to one or other of the **theoretical frameworks**, these are the exception rather than the rule. Most skilled practitioners take an eclectic **approach**: they have an awareness of the strengths and weaknesses of the various **perspectives** and **models**, and they use their professional judgement to select a treatment **approach** most suitable for a given set of circumstances.

CROSS REFERENCE

Chapter 4, Language in use, Top tips, Using a thesaurus

However, caution should be employed when considering the use of **synonyms** (words which have the same or a similar meaning). You should ask yourself if a synonym really has the same meaning as your original word, particularly if you find it in a thesaurus and haven't used it before. If you are unsure, do not be afraid to repeat the original word. In the case of technical terms (such as 'active listening' in Extract A), you should not usually change these at all ('active hearing' or 'careful listening' are not acceptable because they do not reflect conventional usage in the field).

Sometimes a noun can be referred back to with a pronoun (*it, them, him, her, them*, etc), eg:

> **Most skilled practitioners** take an eclectic approach: **they** have an awareness of the strengths and weaknesses of the various perspectives and models, and **they** use **their** professional judgement to select a treatment approach most suitable for a given set of circumstances.

When deciding whether to repeat a noun or replace it with a pronoun, ask yourself if the reader will easily understand what the pronoun refers to. If there is any doubt, repeat the noun.

Task

Noun or pronoun?

 Which choice would help the reader most in the text below? (Remember that one choice can affect the following choice, so there are different ways to make the text coherent. The choices you make are about the whole text, not just one sentence.)

> Fatigue is commonly experienced by people suffering from a variety of chronic illnesses. In the sixteenth century, the concept of 1) <u>fatigue/it</u> was related to a tedious duty; nowadays, 2) <u>fatigue/it</u> is understood as a state of feeling tired for 'no reason'; Barsevick et al. (2010) define 3) <u>fatigue/it</u> as a subjective state, a feeling unrelated to that of being tired after exercise or relieved after rest. 4) <u>Fatigue/It</u> may be regarded as exhaustive, unpredictable in its course, and affecting cognitive ability. 5) <u>Fatigue/It</u> is often described as multidimensional and disabling, affecting the quality of life of those living with it. 6) <u>Fatigue/It</u> is associated with negative emotions such as anxiety, numbness and vulnerability. These are likely to impact on social relationships and family life, often leading to withdrawal and social isolation.
>
> (Adapted from Ormrod and Burns, 2015, p 286)

Referring back in the text: useful words and phrases

There are several examples in the previous texts in this chapter of particular words and phrases commonly used to refer back to 'old' information in the previous sentence:

A

Though there are some practitioners who rigidly adhere to one or other of the theoretical frameworks, **these** are the exception rather than the rule.

B

Midwives should be better trained to support women who are diagnosed with HIV. **This** should include appropriate communication of results, offering individualised support, maintaining confidentiality and providing accurate information on the impact of an HIV positive test. **The latter point** is particularly important …

C

Nowadays, healthcare staff are constantly under pressure to improve services often when resources are stretched. In certain circumstances **this** can result in a communication breakdown or poor provision of care which leads to frustration, particularly when **this** involves patients and relatives who may be anxious and upset, distressed or angry.

D

By collaborating with service users and responding appropriately to their feedback, nurses can deliver more appropriate care and ensure that any concerns raised are dealt with quickly and appropriately (Coulter, 2012). **This** will usually involve collecting and using information provided by patients (e.g. patient satisfaction surveys or focus groups) in order to deliver the kind of services that patients want. **Whichever approach** is used, the key aim is to find out what patients really think about the services we provide and provide supporting evidence of **this**.

These words and phrases can play a huge role in helping the reader to follow the development of a text. Common words and phrases used to refer back are: 'this', 'these', 'the' and 'such'. The words 'this' and 'these' can be used alone (as in some of the examples above), but they (and other words) are often followed by a noun which repeats or summarises information given in the previous sentence. Drummond (2016) has identified the most common 'summary nouns' in academic English as:

- time;
- case;
- point;
- view;
- period;

- process;
- approach;
- question;
- problem;
- area.

Following the process for creating similar lists set out in Drummond (2016), the following nouns with specific reference to medical writing emerge:

- population;
- technique;
- project;
- model;
- patient;
- result;

- sample;
- disease;
- investigation;
- test;
- treatment.

These summary nouns have also been called 'signalling nouns' (Flowerdew, 2003), and indeed, writers often choose to refer back to something with a noun which *signals* their own attitude or stance. For example, 'this problem' is subtly different to 'this challenge', the latter possibly signalling a more positive attitude. What's more, the writer might underline their stance by adding an adjective, such as 'serious' or 'minor' before 'problem'. These choices are part of *criticality*, as they convey the writer's interpretation and stance.

CROSS
REFERENCE

Developing a coherent argument and expressing criticality

Task

Referring back in the text to summarise and comment

1) How does the writer summarise and signal his attitude to something he refers back to in the text below?

> While most people would expect mental health nurses to be involved in helping people on the 'mental health problems' side of the continuum, many are surprised to find (and you may be too) that mental health nurses can be – indeed, are – involved in assisting and supporting people with no history of mental health problems in the maintenance of their mental health. They might do this via various mental health promotion activities, be they direct (such as planning and running work-based stress management programmes or working in a primary care service such as a GP clinic or NHS Direct) or indirect (such as authoring self-help guides in relation to stress or 'common mental health problems' like anxiety and depression). This important aspect of mental health is often overlooked, perhaps because of the dominant stereotypes relating to what mental health nurses do – stereotypes that almost always involve the dishing out of medication or dealing with disturbed individuals in straightjackets.
>
> (Pryjmachuk, 2011, p 7)

2) In the examples below, link back to the ideas in the first sentence using 'this'/'these' and a word from the lists of common summary nouns given earlier in this chapter.

a) The nursing home was closed down for breaching a number of regulations. This _____ was widely reported in the press.

b) Many parents believed that vaccines would cause autism. This _____ is now widely contested.

c) Many homeless people receive little or no health care. The government needs to tackle this serious _____.

d) Different organisations organise nurse rostering in different ways. Whichever _____ is adopted, nurses need to be provided with a clear rationale.

e) This condition can be treated in a number of ways. Whichever _____ is selected, it is important that the patient is carefully monitored.

f) The UN has proposed a number of measures to tackle cholera. This _____ affects millions of people around the world.

3) How do you think the authors of the academic nursing texts below may have referred back to the ideas in the previous sentences to repeat, summarise or comment on an idea?

a) Nurses play an important role in promoting public health. Traditionally, the focus of _____ by nurses has been on disease prevention and changing the behaviour of individuals with respect to their health.

(Kemppainen et al, 2012, p 490)

b) The Lunacy Acts of the mid-nineteenth century essentially created an institutional base for the emerging discipline of psychiatry (Nolan, 1998). Prior to _____, those looking after the mentally ill were often referred to as 'keepers', a somewhat dehumanising term.

(Pryjmachuk, 2011, p 7)

c) If you are administering medication, it is important that you have some pharmacological knowledge about the action of the drug, contraindications, side effects and interactions. You will also need to have knowledge of the usual doses for the drugs you administer so that you can avoid drug errors. Knowledge in _____ ensures not only that you fully understand the actions and the consequences of the drugs that you are administering, but also that you are able to explain these things to patients and their relatives.

(Ward, 2015, p 129)

d) The concept of moral engagement arises from social cognitive theory (Bandura, 1986, 1991) and requires you to stand firm in your moral behaviour, despite the possibility of peer or social pressure to act differently. This takes moral courage. Bandura suggests that a sure way to demonstrate this concept is through empathy. This means you must accept responsibility for your behaviours and demonstrate a humane concern for others at all times. _____ ensures that we are able to consider best practice and best interest for those in our care.

(Lee-Woolf et al, 2015, p 18)

Linking ideas

If the links between ideas are clear and logical, there is often no need to signify them with particular words. In the example below, it is clear that the second sentence explains the reason for the claim in the first sentence.

Another important element of active listening is non-verbal communication. It is widely held that words form only a minor percentage of communication …

Sometimes, **punctuation** alone can be used to signify a link, as in the example below, where a colon is used to signal that what follows is an expansion and explanation.

Most skilled practitioners take an eclectic approach: they have an awareness of the strengths and weaknesses of the various perspectives and models, and they use their professional judgement to select a treatment approach most suitable for a given set of circumstances.

CROSS REFERENCE

Chapter 4, Language in use, Punctuation and sentence structure, Colons

However, often particular words and phrases can be used to signal the relationship between ideas, as in the examples below.

A

While the individual may not have capacity to make some decisions they may still retain capacity for other decisions. **For example** a patient may not have capacity to make a decision regarding a surgical procedure but could retain capacity to consent (or not) to having their clinical observations (eg blood pressure) checked.

B

As far as individual nursing practice is concerned, mental health nurses more often than not adopt the perspective(s) that most appeal to them. **However, given** the current emphasis on evidence-based practice, it is important that we do not let ideological dogma alone dominate our practice.

C

The concept of moral engagement arises from social cognitive theory (Bandura, 1986, 1991) and requires you to stand firm in your moral behaviour, **despite** the possibility of peer or social pressure to act differently.

D

If you are administering medication, it is important that you have some pharmacological knowledge about the action of the drug, contraindications, side effects and interactions.

E

This important aspect of mental health is often overlooked, perhaps **because** of the dominant stereotypes relating to what mental health nurses do

F

This will usually involve collecting and using information provided by patients (e.g. patient satisfaction surveys or focus groups) **in order to** deliver the kind of services that patients want.

G

Though there are some practitioners who rigidly adhere to one or other of the theoretical frameworks, these are the exception rather than the rule.

H

In conclusion, good communication skills lie at the heart of all areas of nursing practice, and can **thus** be considered to be at least as important as the clinical and intellectual skills that a nurse must be proficient in. It is **therefore** important that communication skills are developed and assessed as part of nurse education.

I

In addition to training midwives, support staff (eg receptionists) should **also** be trained to ensure that women's status remains confidential and stigmatisation does not occur.

These linking words and phrases have very specific functions, as demonstrated in the texts above:

- **addition**: in addition to, also
- **exemplification**: for example
- **purpose**: in order to
- **contrast**: while, however, despite, though
- **reason**: because
- **result**: thus, therefore
- **condition**: given, if

This means they are not easily interchangeable. They should not be used as decoration or to make a text 'sound more academic'. In fact, they should only be introduced into the text when the relationship between ideas is not already clear enough.

Certain linking words and phrases can act as explicit **signposts** for the reader, letting them know, for example, why something is included in the text, or what is coming next.

A

One aspect of active listening is verbal communication on the part of the listener such as restating and summarising the speaker's message (Jagger, 2015). **Another important element of active listening is** body language.

B

The aim of this essay is to examine the extent to which communication can be considered to be the **core** nursing skill. **It will begin by** examining what is meant by the term 'communication' in nursing. **It will then** outline what are generally considered to be the core skills required by nurses, with reference to the NMC Code (2015). **It will go on** to examine the impact of communication skills on a range of nursing activities, and assess the role that poor communication has played in a number of documented 'failures' in nursing.

The first example illustrates a structure which is useful for sequencing information and linking new information to a central theme. (Repetition is also important here.) The second example contains typical signposts from essay introductions.

There are clearly many ways to link ideas. The important thing is to make choices based on *meaning*, and the needs of the reader.

Task

Linking ideas

1) Choose the word/phrase which conveys the right meaning in the passages below.

   a) Data were collected on the activities of 25 nurses in a hospital setting. <u>In addition/Moreover</u>, interviews were carried out over a three week period.

   b) A number of overseas nurses reported unacceptable working conditions, particularly in the private sector. <u>In contrast/On the contrary</u>, others praised the NHS for the support it had given them.

   c) A number of nurses may be involved with the patient's family, <u>albeit/however</u> at different times.

   d) Absorption is the process <u>thereby/whereby</u> a drug passes into the body.

   e) The application of heat pads also aids muscle relaxation, <u>hereby/thereby</u> relieving pain.

   f) The report explored the needs of a subgroup of special needs patients, <u>namely/in other words</u>, children and adolescents.

   g) It was reported that most parents had asked to be present for CPR and invasive procedures (64% and 61% <u>respectively/namely</u>).

   h) There are concerns of a 'two-tier' system comprising university-trained nurses and apprenticeship nurses, with <u>the first/the former</u> having more status, and <u>the latter/the last</u> being seen as a cheap option.

2) Delete any linking words or phrases which are unnecessary, do not convey the right meaning, or are grammatically incorrect in the following text.

Asthma is a chronic inflammatory disease of the respiratory system. Furthermore, it is episodic in nature and variable in severity. However, it affects people of all ages. Given that it is also most commonly caused by heightened responsiveness to allergen triggers, resulting in inflammation and narrowing of the airways in affected individuals. While it has been recommended that patients should be fully involved in decisions regarding their treatment. However, a survey conducted by Asthma UK reported that 50% of sufferers had not had a full discussion with a health professional.

(adapted from Cornforthe, 2012)

Developing a coherent argument and expressing criticality

In order to develop a coherent argument, it is necessary to put yourself in the reader's shoes and imagine what the reader will want to know. You must anticipate their questions and guide them carefully through your argument, providing clear signposts so that they don't get lost or stuck. Imagine a very demanding reader!

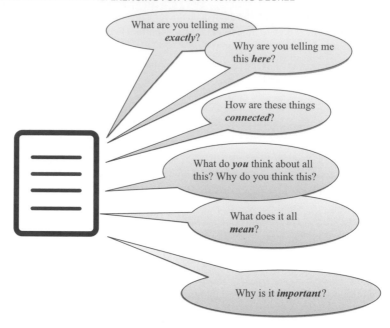

Figure 2.1: Anticipating the reader's questions

Example exam question

Developing a coherent argument

Below is an essay title from a mental health nursing module:

Discuss the role of family intervention strategies in the treatment of psychs.

Read the student's discussion of the background to this issue and consider these questions.

1) Do you find the text easy to follow?
2) How has the student made it easy for you? Have they used any of the patterns discussed in this chapter, such as general/specific information, old/new information, referring back in the text, linking and signposts?
3) Have they guided you through their argument and expressed their stance? How?

Research into psychosis has often focused on the role of the family. In the 1950s (when 'schizophrenia' was the more widely adopted term), the focus appeared to be on the family's role in the **causation** of psychosis. Consider, for example, Lidz et al's notion of 'pathological' families (1965) and the 'double-bind' hypothesis of Bateson et al (1956).

Around the same time as these 'causal' hypotheses were being promoted, the anti-psychotic drugs were discovered. Drugs, by their very nature, are treatments designated for the individual, and this fact, coupled with the prevailing view of families as toxic agents led, unsurprisingly, to what could cynically be called the first family intervention strategy – that of excluding the family.

It is at this point that contradictions emerge. Given that the anti-psychotic drugs were so efficacious at attenuating florid psychotic symptoms, many sufferers were able to avoid the long-term hospitalisations that had hitherto accompanied a diagnosis of schizophrenia. Thus, a policy of closure of the large mental hospitals in favour of community care ensued, a policy that implied – even demanded – that families play a role in the care of their relatives. Families, however, continued to receive scant regard from mental health professionals and policy makers. Denied access to support and advice, families were only useful – indeed, it was deemed they had a responsibility – when hospitals were looking to discharge sufferers into the community. As Bebbington and Kuipers remark, relatives were 'often the only people outside the hospital willing to provide continuing care and shelter for the patient' (1982, p 398).

Not surprisingly, this one-sided attitude frustrated and infuriated families and they began to fight back. The inadequacies of community care that became apparent during the 1970s and 1980s, and relatives' feelings that they were overburdened and being saddled with sufferers without support, soon led to the establishment of self-help groups such as the National Schizophrenia Fellowship (now 'Rethink Mental Illness'). The National Schizophrenia Fellowship (1974a, 1974b; Creer and Wing 1988) argued that it was far more productive for mental health professionals to engage, rather than antagonise, relatives and, as the years went by, mental health professionals and successive governments gradually began to listen.

Discussion: developing a coherent argument

Paragraph 1

Research into psychosis has often focused on the role of the family. In the 1950s (when 'schizophrenia' was the more widely adopted term), the focus **appeared to be** on **the family's role** in the *causation* of the disorder. **Consider, for example**, Lidz et al's notion of 'pathological' families (1965) and the 'double-bind' hypothesis of Bateson et al (1956).

The first paragraph immediately references the task ('psychosis', 'the role of the family'), signalling the relevance of the essay content, and identifying supporting literature ('research into psychosis has often focused on'). It then goes on to establish a clear context for the discussion, suggesting that 'the role of the family' may be more complex than anticipated (the writer's caution with regard to this is expressed in the choice of verb – 'appeared to be'); the italics used for 'causation' serve to suggest a contrast with what the reader might expect. The writer refers the reader to examples from scholars as evidence for the pattern he has identified in the literature (focus on the causal role of the family at that time).

Paragraph 2

Around the same time as **these 'causal' hypotheses** were being promoted, the anti-psychotic **drugs** were discovered. **Drugs, by their very nature**, are treatments designated for the individual, and **this fact, coupled with the prevailing view** of families as toxic agents **led, unsurprisingly, to what could cynically be called** the first family intervention strategy – **that of** excluding the family.

The second paragraph begins by referring back to the idea put forward in the first paragraph with 'these' and a **summary noun** ('these 'causal' hypotheses'), then introduces new information (anti-psychotic drugs were discovered at around the same time). This follows the typical **old/ new** pattern. The second sentence refers back to this new idea through repetition ('drugs'), and then provides an analysis of how the introduction of these drugs led to the exclusion of the family (again following the **old/new** pattern). The writer signals **cause and effect** ('this fact, coupled with … led to'), and explanation ('that of'). His addition of the word 'unsurprisingly' suggests he views the stated effect as an inevitable consequence. Other examples of language which signal the writer's interpretation of the facts are 'by their very nature', 'prevailing' and 'could cynically be called'.

Paragraph 3

It is at this point that contradictions emerge. Given that the anti-psychotic drugs were so efficacious at attenuating florid psychotic symptoms, many sufferers were able to avoid the long-term hospitalisations that had hitherto accompanied a diagnosis of schizophrenia. **Thus**, a policy of closure of the large mental hospitals in favour of community care ensued, a policy that implied – even demanded – that families play a role in the care of their relatives. Families, **however**, continued to receive scant regard from mental health professionals and policy makers. Denied access to support and advice, families were **only** useful – **indeed**, it was deemed they had a responsibility – when hospitals were looking to discharge sufferers into the community. **As Bebbington and Kuipers remark**, relatives were 'often the only people outside the hospital willing to provide continuing care and shelter for the patient' (1982, p 398).

The third paragraph begins with a very explicit **signpost** ('It is at this point that contradictions emerge.'), which clearly signals to the reader that an important stage in the discussion has been reached. Up until this stage, the focus has been on the exclusion of families. This paragraph details how families became important again (but not in a straightforward way, hence the word 'contradictions'). The paragraph then describes a fairly complex set of related factors. It would be easy for the reader to get lost here. However, the writer manages to make everything clear by introducing these factors in a **step-by-step** manner, connecting them through clear chronology and **linking/signposting** language.

1) The patients were able to avoid long-term hospitalisation because of ('given') the drugs.

2) This led to ('thus') the closure of hospitals in favour of community care.

3) But this did not mean ('however') that families were given credit for the new role they were expected to fulfil.

4) In fact, they were undervalued ('*only* useful') and even ('indeed') exploited.

5) Scholars in the literature support this argument ('As Bebbington and Kuipers remark').

Paragraph 4

Not surprisingly, this one-sided attitude **frustrated** and **infuriated** families and they began to **fight** back. The **inadequacies** of **community care** that became apparent during the 1970s and 1980s, and relatives' feelings that they were **overburdened** and being **saddled with** sufferers without support, soon **led to** the establishment of **self-help** groups such as the National Schizophrenia Fellowship (now 'Rethink Mental Illness'). The National Schizophrenia Fellowship (1974a, 1974b; Creer and Wing 1988) **argued** that it was **far more productive** for mental health professionals to **engage, rather than antagonise,** relatives and, as the years went by, mental health professionals and successive governments gradually began to listen.

This paragraph follows a **general-specific** pattern. The first sentence signals the **problem-solution** organisation of the paragraph, and the rest of the paragraph fleshes this out. There is a clear signal of stance at the beginning of the paragraph 4 ('not surprisingly'). The paragraph then refers back to the idea in the previous paragraph with 'this', a **summary noun**, and an adjective which demonstrates a critical stance ('this *one-sided* attitude'). This again follows the **old/new** pattern. The second sentence also refers back to the concept of 'community care' introduced in the previous paragraph, and then proceeds to describe how attitudes and institutions changed over time. Supporting literature is clearly interpreted with the choice of reporting verb ('argued' suggests that something is evidenced and convincing – compare with 'claimed' or 'suggests'). The **problem-solution** organisation is clearly signalled.

- The problem is introduced at the beginning of the paragraph, underpinned with the use of negative words: 'frustrated', 'infuriated', 'fight', 'inadequacies', 'overburdened', 'saddled with'.

- There is then a key causal verb: 'led to'.

- The solution part of the paragraph is characterised by more positive language: 'self-help', 'far more productive', 'engage'.

The language of criticality

When constructing an argument, writers need to use specific language to express their criticality and their stance (Biber, 2006; Argent, 2017). This includes how certain you are about something, how strongly you feel about something, and the extent to which you are convinced by evidence and the opinions of others. Some examples of this type of language use were mentioned in the previous task, eg:

CROSS REFERENCE

Chapter 1, Academic writing: text, process and criticality, Writing critically

- the use of language which explicitly conveys opinion ('by their very nature', 'cynically', 'unsurprisingly', 'saddled with');
- the use of **summary nouns** which convey interpretation or opinion regarding what has been previously mentioned ('these causal hypotheses', 'this one-sided attitude');
- the interpretation of supporting literature through the choice of reporting verbs and expressions ('has often focused on', 'the prevailing view', 'remark', 'argued');
- the use of language which conveys degrees of certainty, especially the use of cautious language to avoid overgeneralisation or unsubstantiated claims ('appeared to be', 'could cynically be called').

Task

Identifying stance

Writers have different views depending on the extent of their knowledge and their interpretation of a situation. How do the following sentences differ in the way the writers assess the situation in question?

1a) This drug will limit the side effects of the treatment.

1b) This drug may limit the side effects of the treatment.

2a) Concerns relating to patient care have been addressed.

2b) Concerns relating to patient care have to some extent been addressed.

3a) The reason for the decline in adolescent smoking is improved education.

3b) The principal reason for the reported decline in adolescent smoking is improved education.

4a) The NHS is currently facing numerous serious problems.

4b) The NHS is currently facing a number of challenges.

5a) Further research is required on this innovative approach.

5b) Further research is required on this largely untested approach.

6a) Campbell argues that changes in funding will impact poorer communities disproportionately.

6b) Brown claims that changes in funding will impact poorer communities disproportionately.

6c) Darcy et al maintain that changes in funding will impact poorer communities disproportionately.

7a) Li et al advocate the use of an elastic support bandage.

7b) Sanders suggests the use of an elastic support bandage.

7c) Clark discourages the use of an elastic support bandage.

8a) All the community nurses share information.

8b) Crucially, all the community nurses share information.

8c) Worryingly, all the community nurses share information.

Discussion: identifying stance

- In 1), 'will' suggests that the writer has been convinced of the certainty of the 'proposition' (ie the drug does x); 'may' suggests uncertainty on the part of the writer regarding the proposition. The writers are clearly assessing the evidence in different ways.

- In 2), 'to some extent' suggests that the writer believes that many concerns have not yet been addressed.

- In 3), 'principal' suggests that the writer believes that there are also other (less important) reasons; the choice of the word 'reported' serves to distance the writer from the claim slightly.

- In 4), 'numerous' means 'many'; 'a number of' means 'some'; the term 'serious problems' suggests a more negative assessment of the situation than 'challenges'.

- In 5), 'innovative' suggests a positive assessment of the situation; 'largely untested' suggests that the writer has concerns.

- In 6), 'argues' suggests that the writer believes Campbell has presented a convincing, well-supported case; 'claims' suggests that the writer sees Brown's view as open to question; 'maintains' suggests that the writer believes Darcy et al are insisting on a view which goes against the majority view or evidence to the contrary.

- In 7), the writers express their interpretation of scholars' views through the choice of verb: 'advocate' means that they strongly recommend something; 'suggest' implies a much weaker recommendation; 'discourage' conveys the opposite of a recommendation.

- In 8), a) is a neutral report of a situation; the addition of the word 'crucially' suggests the writer's belief that this fact is very important or positive; the addition of 'worryingly' suggests the writer's concern about the situation.

Summary

This chapter has looked at the ways in which you can make your writing clear and coherent. It has demonstrated how careful planning and editing can help you to produce a text which a reader can easily navigate and understand. It has shown how to write effective introductions and conclusions, and how to structure clear paragraphs. It has made clear how your choice of language can affect meaning, and impact on the understanding of the reader. It has also demonstrated how arguments can be developed coherently, and expressed through the use of 'critical' language.

Sources of example texts

Burns, D (2015) Leadership and Management. In Burns, D (ed) *Foundations of Adult Nursing*. London: Sage, 205–42.

Cornforthe, A (2012) Management of Asthma Care. *Independent Nurse: For Primary Care and Community Nurses* [online]. Available at: www.independentnurse.co.uk/clinical-article/management-of-asthma-care/63632/ (accessed 10 April 2017).

Kemppainen, V, Tossavainen, K and Turunen, H (2012) Nurse's Roles in Health Promotion Practice: An Integrative Review. *Health Promotion International*, 28(4), 490–501.

Kendal, S and Pryjmachuk S (2011) Helping Young People with Mental Health Difficulties. In Pryjmachuk, S (ed) *Mental Health Nursing: An Evidence-Based Introduction*. London: Sage, 331–61.

Lee-Woolf, E, Jones, J, Brooks, J and Timpson, J (2015) Essentials of Nursing: Values, Knowledge, Skills and Practice. In Burns, D (ed) *Foundations of Adult Nursing*. London: Sage, 3–34.

Lingen-Stallard, A, Furber, C and Lavender, T (2016) Testing HIV Positive in Pregnancy: A Phenomenological Study of Women's Experiences. *Midwifery*, 35, 31–38.

Ormrod, J and Burns, D (2015) Supportive Care: Caring for Adults with Long-term Conditions. In Burns, D (ed) *Foundations of Adult Nursing*. London: Sage, 275–312.

Pryjmachuk, S (2011) Theoretical Perspectives in Mental Health Nursing. In Pryjmachuk, S (ed) *Mental Health Nursing: An Evidence-Based Introduction*. London: Sage, 3–41.

Tierney, P, Freeman, S and Gregory, J (2015) Caring for the Acutely Ill Adult. In Burns, D (ed) *Foundations of Adult Nursing*. London: Sage, 313–60.

Ward, D (2015) The NMC Essential Skills Clusters. In Burns, D (ed.) *Foundations of Adult Nursing*. London: Sage, 109–34.

References

Argent, S (2017) The Language of Critical Thinking [online]. Available at: www.baleap.org/event/eap-northcritical-thinking (accessed 27 February 2017).

Benson, P and Heidish, P (1995) The ESL Expert: Writing Processes and Classroom Practices. In Belcher, D and Braine, G (eds) *Academic Writing in a Second Language: Essays on Research and Pedagogy*. Norwood, NJ: Ablex, 313–30.

Biber, D (2006) Stance in Spoken and Written University Registers. *Journal of English for Academic Purposes*, 5(2), 97–116.

Drummond, A (2016) An Investigation of Noun Frequencies in Cohesive Nominal Groups. *Journal of Second Language Teaching and Research*, 5(1), 62–88.

Flowerdew, J (2003) Signalling Nouns in Discourse. *English for Specific Purposes*, 22(4), 329–46.

Halliday, M and Hasan, R (1976) *Cohesion in English*. London: Longman.

Jordon, R (2001) *Academic Writing Course: Study Skills in English*. 3rd ed. Harlow, Essex: Pearson Education Limited.

Chapter 3
Referring to sources

Learning outcomes

After reading this chapter you will:

- understand the importance of referencing in academic work;
- be aware of different referencing systems;
- be able to apply the Harvard system of referencing in your written work;
- understand how to use sources critically to support your own work and develop your own ideas;
- understand what is meant by the term 'academic malpractice' and learn how to avoid it.

This chapter focuses on referencing, one of the most important academic skills you need to acquire if you are to be successful in your studies. It explains why referencing is so important and how you should go about doing it in your own work. It also discusses how to use sources critically, and how to avoid plagiarism, while illustrating how these two things are often interrelated.

Reflection

1) Why do you think referencing is so important in academic writing?
2) Are you familiar with any particular referencing systems?
3) Have you used any referencing software?
4) What do you think is meant by 'critical' use of sources?

Terminology

The term 'referencing' is generally understood to refer to:

- in-text referencing – the occasions in the main body of a text where you refer to, or quote, the work of others (ie your *sources*);
- the list at the end of the text (usually entitled 'References'), where you list all the sources you have referred to, or quoted, in the text.

In-text references are also sometimes referred to as 'citations', and the verbs 'reference' and 'cite' are both used to refer to the practice of referring to sources.

CROSS
REFERENCE

*Studying for
your Nursing
Degree,*
Chapter 3,
Becoming
a member
of your
academic and
professional
community

Why should I reference?

Accurate referencing of academic work is essential for the following reasons.

- It is a form of academic 'courtesy', both to the writer (by acknowledging their work) and to the reader (by helping them to find the source easily).
- It indicates that you have consulted authorities and checked your facts, allowing the reader to have confidence in what you write.
- It signals that you have contextualised your ideas in a wider framework, linking your work to work done previously by other scholars.
- It shows the reader that you have used the literature to build your own ideas.
- It signals that your ideas are founded upon scholarship, and thus have credibility.
- It signals you, as a writer, are situated within the nursing knowledge community.
- It shows that you are not pretending to be the source of information or ideas found in sources, ie that you are not attempting to **plagiarise**.

How should I reference?

CROSS REFERENCE

Using sources critically

There are two main referencing systems, each named after the universities where they originated:

- The **Harvard** system, sometimes referred to as the 'name-date' or 'author-date' system;
- The **Vancouver** system, sometimes referred to as the 'number' or 'citation-sequence' system.

Both systems are used in health and social care disciplines, and examples of both will be given in this chapter. However, the most commonly used system in nursing degrees is the Harvard system, so this will be analysed in more detail.

The Harvard system

In this system, sources are identified in the main body of the text according to the surname(s) of the author(s) and the publication year of the source, usually separated by a comma. At the end of the text, all references mentioned in the text are presented in **alphabetical order**, according to author surname (or the surname of the first author when there are multiple authors). Note that the reference forms part of the clause or sentence, so comes before any punctuation.

Example (main text)

Most of the available research is either small-scale or descriptive, or is to be found on the periphery of work on other issues that are important to midwives. These include the delivery and organisation of midwifery care (Battersby and Thomson, 1997), the conflicting ideologies present in midwifery practice (Hunter, 2004), the legal considerations of practitioners experiencing stress and bullying (Dimond, 1999, 2002), midwifery supervision (Skoberne, 2003), the midwife-woman relationship (Kirkham, 2000), and the 'emotional labour' of midwifery (Hunter, 2001).

Example (final reference list)

Battersby, S and Thomson, A M (1997) Community Midwives' and General Practitioners' Perspectives, of Antenatal Care in the Community. *Midwifery*, 13, 92–99.

Dimond, B (1999) Stress and the Midwife. *British Journal of Midwifery*, 7, 649–51.

Dimond, B (2002) Staffing, Stress, Bullying and the Midwife. *British Journal of Midwifery*, 10, 710–13.

Hunter, B (2001) Emotion Work in Midwifery: A Review of Current Knowledge. *Journal of Advanced Nursing*, 34, 436–44.

Hunter, B (2004) Conflicting Ideologies as a Source of Emotion Work in Midwifery. *Midwifery*, 20, 261–72.

Kirkham, M (2000) How Can We Relate? In Kirkham, M (ed), *The Midwife–Mother Relationship*. Basingstoke: Palgrave-Macmillan.

Skoberne, M (2003) Supervision in Midwifery Practice. *RCM Midwives Journal*, 6, 66–69.

The Vancouver system

In this system, sources are numbered in the text. The first piece of work you cite becomes reference number 1, the second reference number 2, and so on. At the end of the text, all references mentioned in the text are presented in **numerical order**. Each source only has one number. Thus, if you mention source 1 again later in the text, it retains its number 1, and this is its only number in the final list. Note that the reference forms part of the clause or sentence, so comes before any punctuation.

Example (main body)

Most of the available research is either small-scale or descriptive, or is to be found on the periphery of work on other issues that are important to midwives. These include the delivery and organisation of midwifery care[1], the conflicting ideologies present in midwifery practice[2], the legal considerations of practitioners experiencing stress and bullying[3,4], midwifery supervision[5], the midwife-woman relationship[6], and the 'emotional labour' of midwifery[7].

Example (final list)

1) Battersby, S, Thomson, A M, Community Midwives' and General Practitioners' Perspectives, of Antenatal Care in the Community. *Midwifery*, 1997, 13, 92–99.

2) Hunter, B, Conflicting Ideologies as a Source of Emotion Work in Midwifery. *Midwifery*, 2004, 20, 261–72.

3) Dimond, B, Stress and the Midwife. *British Journal of Midwifery*, 1999, 7, 649–51.

4) Dimond, B, Staffing, Stress, Bullying and the Midwife. *British Journal of Midwifery*, 2002, 10, 710–13.

5) Skoberne, M, Supervision in Midwifery Practice. *RCM Midwives Journal*, 2003, 6, 66–69.

6) Kirkham, M, How Can We Relate? In Kirkham, M (ed), *The Midwife-Mother Relationship*. Palgrave Macmillan, Basingstoke, 2000.

7) Hunter, B, Emotion Work in Midwifery: A Review of Current Knowledge. *Journal of Advanced Nursing*, 2001, 34, 436–44.

Referencing styles

Few health and social care publications use the Vancouver system, although some very prestigious ones do, eg the *British Medical Journal*. The Harvard system is much more common in health and social care, and is used in the *Journal of Advanced Nursing*, the *British Journal of Social Work*, and *Midwifery*, for example.

Within the Harvard and Vancouver systems, there are slight variations between publishers. Each publisher has a particular style – sometimes called a 'house style' – of referencing, ie how they want references presented in their books, journals, etc. This will be a version of either the Harvard or Vancouver systems, with their own particular specifications regarding, for example, the way names are given or the use of commas. This book uses the Harvard system, and examples of Harvard referencing are given in the house style of the book's publisher, Critical Publishing.

A well-known example of a particular style in healthcare disciplines is APA, the style of the American Psychological Association. Your university and your specific department will almost certainly have their own styles: they may adopt a style such as APA, or they may devise their own style. It is essential to know which style is required in a particular assignment. Once you are sure of the requirements, the important thing is to provide references which are **complete**, **accurate** and **consistent**. Some common style variations will be mentioned in the following sections.

Using the Harvard system

In nursing, you will probably be required to use the Harvard system. This section provides general guidelines.

In-text conventions in the Harvard system

In terms of in-text usage, the Harvard system is slightly more complicated than the number system, and there are some conventions that you should be aware of.

Multiple references

When listing multiple sources in the main body of text, it is usually the convention to list them chronologically, with publications from the same year listed alphabetically; they are usually separated with semi-colons, eg:

(Li, 2002; James and Roberts, 2007; Jones; 2007)

If an author has published two works in the same year, the year is followed by a, b etc (explained in more detail later in the chapter), eg:

(Li, 2002b)

CROSS REFERENCE

Compiling your list of references

Direct quotations

Quotations should be used judiciously. Overuse of quotation can be a symptom of an uncritical 'patchwork' use of references, or even plagiarism. You should only quote something if it is particularly interesting or powerful, and it is not always necessary, or most effective, to quote whole sentences (see example below).

In your text:

CROSS REFERENCE

Critical use of sources

- Direct quotations are usually enclosed in 'single' or "double" inverted commas. Follow any guidelines provided on this by your lecturers and be consistent throughout the text.
- A full sentence quotation is introduced with a colon; quoted words or phrases are integrated into your own sentences.
- Page numbers must be provided as part of the reference.
- A quotation must be copied *exactly* as it is written in the book or article from which it has been taken.
- Any words missed out must be indicated by the use of an ellipsis (three dots …). (Sometimes these are enclosed in square brackets to indicate that the omission is yours and not the original author's.)
- Any words inserted or changed (to make the quotation fit in with your own grammar and meaning) must be enclosed in square brackets.
- Long quotations require double indenting and/or a smaller typeface.

CROSS REFERENCE

Academic malpractice

Examples

Longer quote

According to Richie and Lewis (2003, p 185):

> A good focus group is more than the sum of its parts. The researcher harnesses the group process, encouraging the group to work together to generate more in-depth data based on interaction […]. [He or she] helps the group create a reflective environment in which the group can take an issue, approach it as they choose and explore it fully.

Shorter quotes

Richie and Lewis (2003) see a good focus group as 'more than the sum of its parts' (p 185). The researcher facilitates the group dynamic, leading to the generation of 'more in-depth data based on interaction' (p 185).

The use of 'et al'

The Latin phrase 'et al' means 'and others'. In health and social care, it is not uncommon to find articles written by as many as five or more authors. In such circumstances, in-text referencing can get a bit messy, so the format 'first-author et al' is used whenever there are three or more authors.

Note that in the final reference list, you must list *all* of the authors regardless of how many authors there are, unless a house style demands otherwise.

Compiling your final list of references in the Harvard system

The final reference list appears at the end of an assignment, paper or publication, in alphabetical order in the Harvard system. It is usual to precede the list with the simple heading 'References'. This term implies a **one-to-one match** between in-text references and the sources included in the final reference list, ie if a source is in the reference list, it should have been cited in the main body of text and any citation in the main body of text should be listed in the final reference list. The term 'bibliography' is sometimes used in books; it has the wider sense of 'sources of information on this subject' which generally inform a piece of work; this approach is not suitable in an academic assignment, so the term 'references', with its more restricted meaning, is usually required.

There are essentially three main types of hard copy publication you will come across:

- books;
- chapters in edited books;
- journal articles.

In this section, guidelines will be provided on how to reference these and other types of reference. Examples will follow the house style of Critical Publishing, but remember that styles vary, and you will need to find out what is required in your department.

Referencing books

There are two types of book that you will encounter: **standard textbooks**, where the authors have written the entire textbook from beginning to end, and **edited textbooks**, where many different authors have written individual chapters which are subsequently collated by an editor or group of editors. The general format for referencing textbooks is:

Surname[s] of author[s], Initial[s] (Year) *Title: Subtitle*. Edition [if 2nd or greater]. Place of publication: Publisher.

Examples

Bhopal, R (2002) *Concepts of Epidemiology: An Integrated Introduction to the Ideas, Theories, Principles and Methods of Epidemiology*. Oxford: Oxford University Press.

Chenery-Morris, S and McLean, M (2013) *Normal Midwifery Practice*. London: Learning Matters.

Gross, R (2015) *Psychology: The Science of Mind and Behaviour*. 7th ed. London: Hodder Education.

When referring to an edited textbook in its entirety, the abbreviation 'ed' (editor) or 'eds' (editors) is inserted before the publication year.

Examples

Nair, M and Peate, I (eds) (2013) *Fundamentals of Applied Pathophysiology: An Essential Guide for Nursing and Healthcare Students*. 2nd ed. Chichester: Wiley-Blackwell.

Pryjmachuk, S (ed) (2011) *Mental Health Nursing: An Evidence-Based Introduction*. London: Sage.

Referencing chapters in edited books

It is important to distinguish between a straightforward textbook and an edited textbook when referencing. With edited books, different people write the individual chapters and each chapter is treated as a separate article. This means that if students read and make reference to, say, four chapters in an edited book with ten chapters, four references will need to be added to the reference list. The general format for chapters in edited textbooks is:

Surname[s] of chapter author[s], Initial[s] (Year) Title of Chapter. In Surname[s] of editor[s] of book, Initial[s] (ed[s]) *Title of Book: Subtitle of Book*. Edition [if 2nd or greater]. Place of publication: Publisher.

Examples

Blane, D (1991) Inequalities and Social Class. In Scambler, G (ed) *Sociology as Applied to Medicine*. 3rd ed. London: W B Saunders.

Mitchell, K M, Bozarth, J D and Krauft, C C (1977) A Reappraisal of the Therapeutic Effectiveness of Accurate Empathy, Nonpossessive Warmth, and Genuineness. In Gurman, A S and Razin, A M (eds) *Effective Psychotherapy: A Handbook of Research*. Oxford: Pergamon.

Schön, D A (1988) From Technical Rationality to Reflection-in-Action. In Dowie, J and Elstein, A (eds) *Professional Judgement: A Reader in Clinical Decision Making*. Cambridge: Cambridge University Press.

Referencing journal articles

The general format for journal articles is:

Surname[s] of author[s], Initial[s] (Year) Title of Article. *Journal Title*, Volume(Part), Pages.

Examples

Asbury, J (1995) Overview of Focus Group Research. *Qualitative Health Research*, 5(4), 414–20.

Friars, P and Mellor, D (2009) Drop-Out from Parenting Training Programmes: A Retrospective Study. *Journal of Child and Adolescent Mental Health*, 21(1), 29–38.

Hunter, B (2004) Conflicting Ideologies as a Source of Emotion Work in Midwifery. *Midwifery*, 20, 261–72.

Since PDF copies of journal articles are identical to their print counterparts, it is acceptable to reference electronically accessed versions as the print counterpart, since this will provide sufficient information for a reader (or marker) to locate the resource if required.

In addition, the use of the 'digital object identifier' (DOI) – which is a permanent address for documents on the internet – is likely to become more prevalent in the future. Thus, all of the following variants for referencing journal articles are acceptable in student work:

Friars, P and Mellor, D (2009) Drop-Out from Parenting Training Programmes: A Retrospective Study. *Journal of Child and Adolescent Mental Health*, 21(1), 29–38.

Friars, P and Mellor, D (2009) Drop-Out from Parenting Training Programmes: A Retrospective Study. *Journal of Child and Adolescent Mental Health*, 21(1), 29–38. Available at: www.tandfonline.com/doi/pdf/10.2989/JCAMH.2009.21.1.5.807 (accessed 7 January 2015).

Friars, P and Mellor, D (2009) Drop-Out from Parenting Training Programmes: A Retrospective Study. *Journal of Child and Adolescent Mental Health*, 21(1), 29–38. DOI:10.2989/JCAMH.2009.21.1.5.807

Theses and dissertations

Theses and dissertations (for example, PhD and MSc theses) follow a format that is very similar to books, except following the title, [type of thesis], [location of university: name of university] appears, for example:

Smith, H (2007) *Death and the Experiences of Pre-Registration Student Nurses. A Qualitative Investigation*. Unpublished PhD thesis. Leicester: De Montfort University.

Conference proceedings

Conference proceedings are printed documents reflecting the content of a conference. They are dealt with in the same way as chapters in edited textbooks.

Example

Cappanera, P, Scutellà, M G and Visintin, F (2014) Home Care Service Delivery: Equity versus Efficiency in Optimization Models. In Matta, A, Li, J, Sahin, E, Lanzarone, E and Fowler, J (eds) *Proceedings of the International Conference on Health Care Systems Engineering.* New York, NY: Springer.

Newspapers and magazines

Occasionally, you might need to reference an article in a newspaper or magazine, but bear in mind the quality of the newspaper or magazine being used. The format for newspapers and magazines is much the same as for journal articles, except that the full date of the issue is required.

Example

Marks, N (2014) Guardian Readers Reveal what Makes them Happy at Work. *The Guardian,* 11 June [online]. Available at: www.theguardian.com/sustainable-business/happy-work-what-makes-you www.theguardian.com/sustainable-business/happy-work-what-makes-you (accessed 25 October 2016).

Organisational or 'corporate' authors

Institutions and organisations produce many papers and documents. These often cause referencing problems. Remember, however, that these institutions and organisations can be authors in their own right and thus it is fairly easy to reference material by these bodies as the name you need for a name-year system is simply the organisation's name.

So, the Department of Health, the Royal College of Nursing, the NMC, can all be cited as authors – Department of Health (1991), RCN (1987), NMC (2002), for example.

Examples

Department of Health (2013) *The NHS Constitution for England: The NHS Belongs to us all.* London: Department of Health.

National CAMHS Review (2008) *Children and Young People in Mind: The Final Report of the National CAMHS Review.* London: Department for Children, Schools and Families/Department of Health.

National Schizophrenia Fellowship (1974) *Social Provision for Sufferers from Chronic Schizophrenia.* Surbiton: NSF.

NMC (2015) *The Code: Professional Standards of Practice and Behaviour for Nurses and Midwives.* London: NMC.

Common problems in referencing

'Anonymous' authors

With some documents, such as dictionaries or Acts of Parliament, it is difficult to find out who the author is. In these cases, it is acceptable to reference by the document or series title.

Examples

Collins English Dictionary (2011) 11th ed. Glasgow: William Collins & Sons.

Mental Capacity Act (2005) London: HMSO.

Authors with multiple outputs in the same year

Some authors produce several publications in one year. If two or more articles are attributed to the same author or group of authors in a particular year, you need to use some means of distinguishing between the articles. For example, if you use three papers written by Dianne Jones and published in 2004 in an assignment, how would a reader know which paper 'Jones (2004)' refers to? It could be any of the three. (This isn't a problem with Vancouver-style approaches as you would give each paper a separate number as you used it.)

The way to do this in the Harvard system is to use alphabetical sequencing (a, b, c, etc) to distinguish between the articles. So you call the first paper you use Jones (2004a), the second, Jones (2004b), the third, Jones (2004c). The references in the final list would therefore be:

Jones, D (2004a) [Title, etc of first Jones paper you cite.]

Jones, D (2004b) [Title, etc of second Jones paper you cite.]

Jones, D (2004c) [Title, etc of third Jones paper you cite.]

Note that *you*, as the writer, have inserted the letters a, b, c after the publication year. They are not fixed like the publication year, but serve only to distinguish between the three 2004 Jones articles you are using. If you only used one of the Jones papers, you would not need to use any letters after the publication year.

Secondary citations

Sometimes, students make use of references they find in books and articles they have been reading, but do not actually consult the original sources. To present these secondary references as primary references is really a form of academic malpractice. To avoid this, you should ideally follow up the secondary references and consult the original sources. Where this is genuinely not possible, you can make use of the phrases 'cited in' or 'cited by' to acknowledge that the reference is a secondary reference. Secondary references are usually presented as follows:

In the text

(Jones and Johnston, 1999, cited in Pryjmachuk and Richards, 2007)

In the list of references

Pryjmachuk S and Richards D A (2007) Predicting Stress in Pre-registration Nursing Students. *British Journal of Health Psychology*, 12, 125–44.

Electronic sources of information

Increasingly, students are making use of electronic sources of information such as the Internet, e-journals and PDF documents when undertaking assignments. Providing that the information employed is in a legitimate format and from a legitimate source (eg a reputable organisation), such information can be extremely valuable. For in-text referencing, the format for electronic sources of information is very much the same as for hard copy material, ie you need a name and a publication year. For compiling the final reference list, the format for referencing electronic material is similar to the format for books and journal articles, except that some additional information is required:

- The type of medium – webpage, PDF, DVD, computer program, etc. – is required (in square brackets) after the resource/document details.
- Following the type of medium, use the phrase 'Available at' or 'Available from' followed by information about the source of the material used, eg the specific computer program, web page, etc.
- The access date (in brackets) is required after the source.
- If no creation/publication date is available for the electronic material, simply write 'no date' where the publication year would normally go.
- If no author can be found, follow the guidance given above for anonymous authors.

Examples

Merriam-Webster Dictionary [online]. Available at: www.merriam-webster.com (accessed 15 May 2017).

Nursing and Midwifery Council (2015) *The Code: Professional Standards of Practice and Behaviour for Nurses and Midwives* [online]. Available at: www.nmc.org.uk/globalassets/sitedocuments/nmc-publications/nmc-code.pdf (accessed 15 May 2017).

There is still debate about how to reference electronic material correctly so don't worry too much about any minor differences in approaches that you come across.

Variations in referencing

Although referencing systems are dependent on some set rules, there is a degree of flexibility, mainly brought about by differences in the house styles of various publishers and organisations. The important thing is to follow guidelines and to make sure that your references are complete, accurate and consistent – don't mix and match in the same piece of work. The following variations are common in the Harvard system:

In-text

- A comma is usual between the name and date, but is sometimes omitted, eg (Thomas 2016) rather than (Thomas, 2016).
- Page numbers for direct quotes can be either preceded by a comma and 'p' or 'p.' ('pp' or 'pp.' for a page range), or by a colon, eg (Thomas, 2016, p. 36) or (Thomas, 2016: 36).
- The phrase 'et al' is sometimes written 'et al.' or '*et al.*'.

Final list

- For journal articles, **bold** is often used to indicate volumes, eg:

  Friars, P and Mellor, D (2009) Drop-Out from Parenting Training Programmes: A Retrospective Study. *Journal of Child and Adolescent Mental Health*, **21**(1), 29–38.

- Page numbers are sometimes preceded by p/pp or p./pp.
- Initials are often followed with full stops to indicate the abbreviation, eg:

  Pryjmachuk, S. (ed) (2011) *Mental Health Nursing: An Evidence-Based Introduction*. London: Sage.

- Full first names are sometimes used instead of initials, eg:

  Pryjmachuk, Steven (ed) (2011) *Mental Health Nursing: An Evidence-Based Introduction*. London: Sage.

- The abbreviations 'ed' and 'eds' are often followed by full stops – 'ed.', 'eds.'
- Titles can be in lower case (apart from the first word and proper nouns), or they can be capitalised throughout (apart from 'grammar' words such as prepositions and pronouns), or they can distinguish between titles and subtitles, eg:

  Swales, J and Feak, C (2012) *Academic writing for graduate students: essential tasks and skills.* 3rd ed. Michigan: Michigan ELT.

  Swales, J and Feak, C (2012) *Academic Writing for Graduate Students: Essential Tasks and Skills*. 3rd ed. Michigan: Michigan ELT.

  Swales, J and Feak, C (2012) *Academic Writing for Graduate Students: Essential tasks and skills*. 3rd ed. Michigan: Michigan ELT.

Task

Referencing errors

1) Below are a number of entries than might appear in a text. What problems can you identify and correct?

 a) According to Tarrier and Barrowclough, carers need information, and professionals have a moral duty to supply it.

 b) The major hindrance appears to be the cultural dominance of 'technical rationality'. Schön 1988.

 c) In a theoretical paper, Dickoff and James (1968) argue this position, which is subsequently backed up by a further, data-based paper (Dickoff and James 1968).

 d) Meleis [2001] speculates that historical and cultural paternalism are largely to blame.

e) To quote from Benner 1984: Expertise develops when the clinician tests and refines propositions, hypotheses and principle-based expectations in actual practice situations.

f) According to Green, H (2016) women are the primary carers in society.

g) The results are consistent with the findings of Posner, Wilson and Kraj (2012).

h) Smith [cited by Jones 2014] suggests that the findings are incomplete.

i) … (see, for example, Lewin's 'change spiral' in his book of 1958).

j) (Schön 1988) suggests that this paradox can be resolved by acknowledging the importance of subjectivity.

2) Below are a number of entries than might appear in a final reference list. What problems can you identify and correct?

a) Robert W Smith (1996) PSYCHOLOGY AND HEALTH CARE. London: Ballère Tindall.

b) Weleminsky, J *Schizophrenia and the family: the customers' view*. International Review of Psychiatry, 3, 119–24, 1991.

c) Stevens, B J (1984) Nursing Theory: Analysis, Application and Evaluation. 2nd edition.

d) D Richards et al (2005) Specialist educational intervention for acute inpatient mental health nursing staff: service user views and effects on nursing quality. J. Adv. Nurs., [51], 634–644.

e) Lindsay, B (1991) The gap between theory and practice. Nursing Standard.

f) Calman and Royston (1997) *Risk language and dialects*. BMJ, 315.

g) Reducing re-offending by ex-prisoners. Social Exclusion Unit, London (2002).

h) Parsonage et al (2012) https://www.centreformentalhealth.org.uk/liaison-psychiatry-nhs [accessed 14 May].

Top tips

Referencing software

There are a number of referencing software packages that you may choose to use, eg **Endnote**, **Mendeley**, **Zotero** and **Papyrus**, but this is a purely personal decision. They have advantages: they ensure that there is always a one-to-one match between your in-text references and those listed in the final reference list; you can switch automatically and painlessly between different house styles (even between Harvard and Vancouver). They also have disadvantages: you may not be able to get the software on your home computer without buying it (and it can be quite expensive); their integration into word processing packages can be problematic, causing formatting glitches, for example.

Using sources critically

It is important to know the rules for referencing, but this is just part of the bigger picture. Many students feel confused about referencing. Look at the typical comments below. Do you ever feel like this?

Case studies

1) 'I worry about using too many references. I think it won't be my ideas in the essay.'

2) 'I found a lot of good quotes for my essay, but the lecturer said it was too descriptive and that I didn't have an argument.'

3) 'I spent ages paraphrasing – changing every word of the original text so that I don't plagiarise and get into trouble. But the lecturer didn't think I had understood the ideas in the literature. She also said my language was "awkward".'

4) 'I found lots of opinions on this subject but I don't know how to make them into an essay.'

5) 'The lecturer said I should give my own opinion, but I'm worried that I'm not as expert as the people writing in books and journals.'

These concerns are understandable. Using sources critically is one of the biggest challenges of university study, and well-meaning advice can often appear contradictory. Firstly, it is important to understand that using references is not a negative thing. On the contrary, it is a positive thing, as it shows you have researched the topic. However, in order for references to enhance your work, they must be used *critically*. Table 3.1 illustrates exactly what this means.

Table 3.1: Critical use of sources

UNCRITICAL USE OF SOURCES	CRITICAL USE OF SOURCES
Other voices dominate your essay.	References to other scholars support your voice, but don't replace it.
You mostly *describe* the contents of the literature; you mostly engage in 'knowledge-*telling*' (Beirerter and Scardamalia, 1987).	You describe, *analyse* and *evaluate* the contents of the literature; you engage in 'knowledge-*transforming*', ie *doing* something with knowledge (Beirerter and Scardamalia, 1987).
You use paraphrase to report what scholars say, staying quite close to the original text and replacing individual words with synonyms (to avoid plagiarism).	You demonstrate understanding by paraphrasing in your own words. You try to convey the sense of the sources you refer to, or to interpret them, in a way that supports your argument and acts as a springboard for your own ideas.
There is an over-reliance on quotation. You build your essay around impressive quotations which you think speak for themselves.	You *explain* quotations and integrate them into your own argument; you use quotations to build, support and underline arguments.
You provide a 'patchwork' of references, merely reporting what each individual says, without considering how sources relate to each other or to your argument.	Sources are grouped according to common threads, or compared and contrasted.
You present sources in a random order.	You identify developments, patterns and relationships in the literature, and this determines their place in your essay.
You expect the reader to make the connection between the literature and the context of the assignment.	You explicitly relate what you find in the literature to the context of the assignment; you establish a clear link between your work and the work previously done by other scholars, showing how it has helped you build your ideas.

Advanced skills

Originality

The concept of originality is often misunderstood. It does not mean that you spontaneously make up your own theory or come up with a brand new idea. It means treating the topic in question in a way that is *unique to you*, perhaps finding a new way of looking at something. This usually entails appraising viewpoints and evidence on a specific topic or issue, and coming up with your own ideas about it based on what you have been convinced by. To be credible, academic work should be grounded in the literature of your discipline, as knowledge can only really advance – in your mind or in the discipline as a whole – if it is based on and builds on what has gone before. So the work and ideas of other scholars should of course feature heavily in your work. However, the strongest voice in your work should always be your own. If you can approach what you read and hear critically, and use the ideas of others not only to explore an area of knowledge, but also to inform and shape your own argument, you will be making an original contribution to the subject.

Task

Critical use of sources

Which texts best demonstrate critical use of sources? How?

A

Kessler et al (2005) state that mental health problems in the general population frequently commence in adolescence. School-based services for early identification and intervention and for care coordination in primary care are advocated in the USA (Taras, 2004) and many other European countries (Braddick et al, 2009).

B

As mental health problems in the general population frequently commence in adolescence (Kessler et al, 2005), there is a strong case for embedding the skills of recognition and basic management into wider health and education services. Indeed, school-based services for early identification and intervention and for care coordination in primary care are advocated in the USA (Taras, 2004) and in many other European countries (Braddick et al, 2009).

C

There have been a number of studies investigating women's views on the acceptability of the antenatal HIV test in pregnancy (Duffy et al, 1998; Simpson et al, 1998; Boyd et al, 1999). However, there are limited in-depth explorations of pregnant women's experiences. Existing literature tends to focus on issues such as mothering (Sandelowski and Barroso, 2003), decision-making (Kirshenbaum et al, 2004) and psychological impact (Nancy et al, 2004). Previous qualitative research has looked at pregnant women who were unaware of their HIV-positive status. Sanders, for example, presented powerful narratives of nine HIV-positive women's experiences of temporarily losing parental rights, and of how mothering positively impacted on their recovery.

D

There have been a number of studies investigating women's views on the acceptability of the antenatal HIV test in pregnancy (Duffy et al, 1998; Simpson et al, 1998; Boyd et al, 1999). Sandelowski and Barroso (2003) focus on mothering. Kirshenbaum et al (2004) focus on decision-making. Nancy et al (2004) look at psychological impact. Sanders presents powerful narratives of nine HIV-positive women's experiences of temporarily losing parental rights, and of how mothering positively impacted on their recovery.

E

Cotgrove (2007) questions the effectiveness of psychological therapies for young people with depression such as CBT and family therapy, and claims that antidepressants have better outcomes. Timini (2007) believes that most childhood distress is self-limiting and does not require extensive intervention. He questions the effectiveness of antidepressants, claiming that scientific accuracy is being sacrificed to marketing spin, and that there may be a link between antidepressants and suicide.

F

There is some debate regarding the use of antidepressants to treat young people. On the one hand, Cotgrove (2007) points to evidence showing the benefits of treatment with antidepressants. He suggests that these treatments are more effective than psychological therapies for young people with depression such as CBT and family therapy. In contrast, Timini (2007) questions the effectiveness of antidepressants, claiming that scientific accuracy is being sacrificed to marketing spin, and even going so far as to suggest a link between antidepressants and suicide. In fact, he questions whether intervention is always necessary, believing that most childhood distress is by nature self-limiting.

Discussion: critical use of sources

Texts A, D and E simply repeat what the literature says – the writer's voice is not apparent; text B (Pryjmachuk et al, 2011) uses the literature to support an argument ('As … there is a strong case for … Indeed …'). Text C (adapted from Lingen-Stallard et al, 2016, p 32) identifies common threads ('limited in-depth explorations of'; 'Existing literature tends to focus on'; 'Previous qualitative research has looked at') and contrasts ('existing' v 'previous'). Text F (student writing) identifies a clear contrast ('on the one hand', 'in contrast'), and the writer's voice is clearly driving the text ('There is some debate', 'even going so far as', 'in fact').

One simple aspect of criticality in source use is the focus that the writer affords information. One of the ways this expresses itself is in the use of **author-prominent** or **information-prominent** sentences. When a writer uses an author-prominent sentence, they place some degree of importance on *who* has written something, as well as what they have written, and the author's name forms part of the sentence structure, eg:

> In contrast, <u>Timini</u> (2007) questions the effectiveness of antidepressants

When a writer uses an information-prominent sentence, they focus primarily on *what* is being said, and the author's name is only mentioned in the reference, eg:

> As mental health problems in the general population frequently commence in adolescence (<u>Kessler</u> et al, 2005)

In texts B and C, there is a clear focus on information, reflected in the information-prominent sentences. In F (and even E), there is a focus on key players in an important debate. Texts A and D use a mixture of information- and author-focused sentences, but their use appears to be quite random.

Task

Focus

 1) Identify which of the sentences below are:
- author-prominent;
- information prominent.

 2) In author prominent sentences, a writer can convey their view of a scholar's ideas with the verbs or expressions they choose to use to report them. Which verbs and expressions are used in the author-prominent examples?

   a) As Wright (1993) points out, one of the paradoxes of successful change is that it escapes public notice simply because it is successful.

   b) One of the paradoxes of successful change is that it escapes public notice simply because it is successful (Wright, 1993).

   c) According to Scheidlinger and Aronson (2001), group therapy has been used to treat a wide range of symptomolotalogy in adolescents.

   d) Group therapy has been used to treat a wide range of symptomolotalogy in adolescents (Scheidlinger and Aronson, 2001).

   e) Thomas et al (2013) argue that nursing will only really develop as a profession if nurses become more political.

   f) Nursing will only really develop as a profession if nurses become more political (Thomas et al, 2013).

3) Listed below are some verbs commonly used by writers to convey their understanding and interpretation of the literature.

acknowledge; advocate; argue that; identify; define something as; distinguish between

Below are some nursing texts, followed by a student's paraphrase. Choose the best verb from the list above to complete each paraphrase so that it conveys the sense of the original text.

A

Text

Midwives are crucial in improving the experience of women when they test HIV positive and to do this they need to be appropriately trained. Midwives need to acknowledge the social and psychological impact of HIV and pathways should be developed to support early referral for appropriate support.

(Lingen-Stallard et al, 2016, p 31)

Paraphrase

Lingen-Stallard et al (2016) _____ targeted training for midwives dealing with HIV positive women.

B

Text

Following data analysis, four principal themes emerged from the data, each containing several subthemes.

(Pryjmachuk et al, 2011, p 852)

Paraphrase

Pryjmachuk et al (2011) _____ four principle themes.

C

Text

Like most qualitative findings, elements may only be transferrable to similar contexts.

(Lingen-Stallard et al, 2016, p 37)

Paraphrase

Lingen-Stallard et al (2016) _____ the limitations of the study.

D

Text

Postnatal depression may be mild or severe. While milder forms might be treated within the primary healthcare team, more severe forms will need additional input from psychiatric services.

(Adapted from Taylor, 2015, p 145)

Paraphrase

Taylor (2015) _____ mild and severe forms of postnatal depression.

E

Text

One of the original critical nursing decision makers who pursued a notion of nursing care delivery that was not in keeping with the culture of the time was Florence Nightingale.

(Cooke, 2015, p 182)

Paraphrase

Cooke _____ Florence Nightingale was a pioneer of 'critical nursing decision makers' (2015, p 182).

F

Text

Diabetes Mellitus is a chronic and lifelong condition which occurs when an individual's blood glucose becomes elevated.

(Ormrod and Burns, 2015, p 282)

Paraphrase

Ormrod and Burns _____ 'a chronic and lifelong condition which occurs when an individual's blood glucose becomes elevated' (2015, p 282)

Academic malpractice

Academic malpractice includes any practice whereby a student attempts to gain credit that they do not deserve. Academic malpractice is a disciplinary offence in almost all universities and it can have severe consequences. The most common types of academic malpractice are:

- **plagiarism** – using the ideas, work or words of others without clear acknowledgement;
- **collusion** – hiding the contribution of others in your work;
- **falsification** – or fabrication of results.

Most written assignments are screened using software such as **Turnitin**. Turnitin alerts lecturers to possible instances of plagiarism or collusion. Work that shows a significant match with the literature or with an essay by another student will be closely scrutinised by assessors. Serious and/or repeated incidences of plagiarism/collusion will be penalised (a mark of zero is typical, sometimes without an option to resubmit) and may also lead to a disciplinary hearing.

Avoiding academic malpractice is especially important in those studying for a professional qualification, as professional bodies (eg the NMC) insist on a person's integrity if they are to enter, or remain on, the appropriate professional register. To enter and remain on the NMC Register, a person needs to be of 'good health and good character', and intentional academic malpractice is likely to be seen an impediment to good character.

Just as if you were a qualified nurse, charges of malpractice while a student are likely to lead to you being hauled before a disciplinary or 'Fitness to Practice' committee and you could be expelled from the university – and your professional course – if found guilty. These committees are very formal and tend to include the presence of very senior members of the university, and even lawyers.

Top tips

Avoiding plagiarism

Plagiarism can be a result of someone's clear intention to cheat, but often it can arise from a misunderstanding of academic culture and referencing conventions. Always remember the following.

- Acknowledge the sources of *all* information and ideas, whether directly quoted or paraphrased. References are a good thing: they show you have researched the topic, and, used well, they don't detract from your ideas or originality, they enhance them.
- Overuse of quotation can be seen as a type of plagiarism, and it is certainly a symptom of uncritical use of sources. Only quote something if it is particularly interesting or powerful. Think about using effective words and phrases, integrated into your own words, rather than a whole sentence.
- The more you explain and interpret the literature, and the more you integrate it into your own argument and use it to suit your own writing purpose, the less likely you are to plagiarise. Plagiarism is more likely to occur with a 'patchwork' presentation of sources.

Summary

This chapter has explained why and how you should reference. It has outlined the main features of the Harvard system of referencing, and highlighted some common problems encountered by students. It has guided you towards using sources in a critical way to enhance your own writing, and it has examined the issue of academic malpractice and suggested strategies which can help you to avoid it.

Sources of example texts

Cooke, M (2015) Clinical Decision Making. In Burns, D (ed) *Foundations of Adult Nursing*. London: Sage, pp 179–204.

Lingen-Stallard, A, Furber, C and Lavender, T (2016) Testing HIV Positive in Pregnancy: A Phenomenological Study of Women's Experiences. *Midwifery*, 35, 31–38.

Ormrod, J and Burns, D (2015) Supportive Care: Caring for Adults with Long-Term Conditions. In Burns, D (ed) *Foundations of Adult Nursing*. London: Sage.

Pryjmachuk, S, Graham, T, Haddad, M and Tylee, A (2011) School Nurses' Perspectives on Managing Mental Health Problems in Children and Young People. *Journal of Clinical Nursing*, 21, 850–59. Available at: www.ncbi.nlm.nih.gov/pubmed/21883575 (accessed 15 May 2017).

Taylor, G (2015) Exposure to Other Fields of Nursing. In Burns, D (ed) *Foundations of Adult Nursing*. London: Sage.

References

Beirerter, C and Scardamalia, M (1987) *The Psychology of Written Composition*. Hillsdale, NJ: Lawrence Erlbaum.

Nursing and Midwifery Council (2015) *The Code: Professional Standards of Practice and Behaviour for Nurses and Midwives*. Available at: www.nmc.org.uk/globalassets/sitedocuments/nmc-publications/nmc-code.pdf (accessed 15 May 2017).

Chapter 4
Language in use

Learning outcomes

After reading this chapter you will:

- have gained knowledge of academic style;
- have developed strategies for improving the clarity of your writing;
- be able to distinguish between formal and informal language with confidence;
- have gained knowledge of useful grammar and punctuation rules and patterns in academic writing;
- be able to avoid some common errors in academic writing.

This chapter provides information and strategies to help develop your control of language for the purpose of academic writing. It will help you to write clearly, and to produce writing which is accurate and academic in style.

Reflection

1) What do you understand by 'academic style'?

2) What challenges do you face when you try to write in an academic style?

3) Are there any aspects of grammar, spelling and punctuation that you struggle with?

4) What resources do you use to help you with writing?

Academic style

You will hear a lot about 'academic style' and 'academic writing' at university. It can sometimes feel as if you are expected to learn a new language, or a different version of the English you know. This can be intimidating, especially if you do not have a lot of recent experience in writing academic essays, or if English is not your first language. Of course, it is necessary to adopt an appropriate style at university, particularly in writing, but there is nothing mysterious about this style. In fact, it could be said to have just three basic characteristics:

- it is clear and easy to read;
- it is concise and precise;
- it is formal in expression.

CROSS
REFERENCE

Chapter 2,
Coherent texts
and arguments

Clarity

The information, ideas and arguments you are required to present in academic essays may be very complex. It is therefore particularly important that the language you use to communicate these things is as clear and readable as possible. As mentioned above, many factors contribute to clarity, some of which will be discussed in this section, some of which are covered in other parts of this book. Clarity and coherence, in particular, are inextricably linked, so you will find many cross references to Chapter 2.

Task

Clarity

Read the two paragraphs below and decide which is clearer and easier to read.

A

As McGrandels and Duffy (2012) point out, a degree of anxiety and worry is a normality for most people, who will feel anxiety at some point in their lives. People feel stressed and the heart rate increases and blood pressure rises and there is diversion of blood to the muscles for 'fight or flight' initiation, like running away. People are careful and prepared for dealing with short-term menacing threats and difficult emergencies (Wilkinson, 2005) and there is enhancement of energy from a rise in blood sugar from a release of a chemical called cortisol into the blood stream by the adrenal glands.

B

As McGrandels and Duffy (2012) point out, a degree of anxiety is normal and most people will experience anxiety at some point in their lives. Anxiety and stress can initiate protective mechanisms in the body which prepare us for 'fight of flight'. When this happens, the heart rate increases, blood pressure rises, and blood is diverted to the muscles to help us respond to the threat, by running away, for example. Cortisol is also released into the blood stream by the adrenal glands, and this has the effect of raising blood sugar in order to enhance energy. The result of this response is increased vigilance and a preparedness to deal with short-term threats and emergencies (Wilkinson, 2005).

Discussion: clarity

Text B is taken (in a slightly adapted form) from a widely used nursing text book (Taylor, 2015, p 168). You probably found it easier to read than Text A. There are a number of reasons for this.

- Overall, Text B **flows**, whereas Text A is meandering and disjointed, and the reader has to work hard to extract any sense from it. Text B is kinder to the reader: it moves from a general statement in the first sentence to specific details. It explains a complex process step by step, whereas A jumps around from one part of the process to another in a random fashion. In B, the stages are logically ordered and clearly linked, in this case reflecting real-life biological processes. Linking words such as 'also' in B are a way of making connections explicit.

- It is common in English writing to refer back to the main theme of the previous sentence before introducing new information. This can be seen in B, in the use of the word 'anxiety' in the first sentence and then at the start of the second sentence, and in the use of the phrases 'when this happens' and 'the result of this response' later in the text; 'this/these' are commonly used to refer back in a text.

- Text B uses repetition to help the reader. For example, as noted above, the second sentence repeats the word 'anxiety' from the first sentence; Text A breaks this link and starts talking about people feeling 'stressed', which is a slightly different point. In A, the reader gets confused, or has to make a connection for themselves, and no reader should have to work that hard!

- Text B has shorter sentences which contain a manageable amount of information; Text A sometimes tries to cover too much information in a single sentence, and it overuses the word 'and' to connect ideas in a very loose way.

- Text B uses simple, direct language: 'normal', rather than 'normality'; 'blood is diverted' rather than 'there is diversion of blood'; 'to deal with' rather than 'for dealing with'; 'to enhance' rather than 'there is enhancement of'.

- Text B is concise. It does not include unnecessary words or phrases. In A, there is redundancy, ie the use of two or more words which actually mean the same or very similar things ('anxiety and worry'), and the inclusion of words which are unnecessary because they do not add meaning ('threats' are by definition 'menacing'; 'emergencies' imply 'difficulty').

- Text B uses more precise expression. We conventionally 'experience' – rather than 'have' – anxiety, and the word 'vigilant' (being careful to look out for particular dangers) carries much more specific meaning than the rather vague 'careful'.

CROSS
REFERENCE

Chapter 2,
Coherent
texts and
arguments,
General and
specific
information

Strategies for achieving clarity

From the previous discussion of the two texts, it is clear that there are certain strategies that you can adopt to help you produce clearer writing.

1) Order ideas and sentences in a logical, step-by-step manner, moving from **general to specific** information and ideas.

2) Consider if it will help the reader if you **link back** to the previous sentence before introducing new information, possibly using 'this/these'.

3) Use sensible **repetition** to remind the reader of what is being discussed. This can be seen as a kind of 'lucid repetition' because of how it may facilitate the brain's ability to process information (McIntyre, 1997); note that this is quite different from redundancy, where words or information are repeated for no good reason, often because the text is insufficiently controlled.

CROSS
REFERENCE

Chapter 2,
Coherent
texts and
arguments,
Old and new
information

4) Do not be afraid of using **short sentences** and **simple language** where these help you communicate difficult ideas clearly. Most academic writing contains a mixture of short and long sentences, but it is important that long sentences are carefully constructed, and that they are not just chains of phrases linked by 'and' or 'but'.

5) Be **concise**. Avoid redundancy and wordiness – throwing down words on the page for their own sake does not make something more academic! Also, remember that you will be required to meet strict word counts in your essays.

6) Be **precise**. Choose words and expressions very carefully so that they convey the exact message you intend. Check that your expression is not vague or ambiguous.

Task

CROSS
REFERENCE

Chapter 2,
Coherent
texts and
arguments,
Referring back
in the text:
repetition,
variation and
pronoun use

Being concise

 Cross out any unnecessary words (ie words which are redundant or which do not add meaning) in the text below.

Mary Seacole was born in the country of Jamaica in the year 1805. She studied and learned about herbal medicine in the country of Jamaica. She was also well travelled, and during her travels to different places, she acquired a great deal of knowledge on medicine and drugs and caring for the sick. Like her contemporary of the same time, Florence Nightingale, she petitioned people in the British government to send her to Crimea to help and assist in the army military hospital. The country's government declined her request, but she decided to fund her own visit by herself with her own money. In Crimea, she nursed sick and wounded soldiers. Seacole died in the year 1910. Her contribution to medicine went unrecognised while she was alive but, in 1991, she was posthumously awarded the Jamaican Order of Merit after her death, and in 2004, she came top of a poll to decide the 'greatest black Briton'. She is considered by many people to be a pioneer of nursing.

Task

Being precise

Choose the word or phrase which conveys the most precise meaning in the sentences below.

1) Over the course of the last century, nursing <u>grew/evolved</u> into a highly skilled profession.

2) Minimally <u>invasive/intrusive</u> surgery is becoming increasingly common.

3) The study surveyed nurses to <u>determine/decide</u> their reasons for entering the profession.

4) Those patients <u>having/exhibiting</u> symptoms of cholera were placed under immediate quarantine.

5) Nurses will <u>administer/give</u> drugs at local clinics.

6) The study reports on a simple <u>diagnosis/diagnostic</u> test for cystic fibrosis.

7) Improved medicine management has a high impact <u>for/in terms of</u> patient satisfaction.

8) The report details the side effects <u>of/associated with</u> the treatment.

Top tips

Being precise

Avoid using 'etc' or 'and so on'. Also avoid ending sentences with ellipsis (…). Instead use 'such as' or 'for example/for instance' with two or three concrete examples.

The study looks into the factors affecting blood pressure – obesity, smoking etc.

→ The study looks into the factors affecting blood pressure such as obesity and smoking.

Formality

Everybody changes their language to suit the situation they are in: they speak politely and carefully in a job interview; they use relaxed – or sometimes colourful – language among friends; the tone of their emails varies, depending on the recipient.

Task

Identifying formal style

Look at the texts below and decide if they are formal or informal. What is the purpose of each text? Who do you think is the target reader?

A

Postpartum (or puerperal) psychosis is a severe episode of mental illness representing a psychiatric emergency, with a sudden onset during the days or weeks following childbirth. (Royal College of Psychiatrists, 2014). It is more serious than postnatal depression and can present in different ways. Affected women may have very rapid changes in mood, including symptoms of depression or mania (Royal College of Psychiatrists, 2014). A woman with postpartum psychosis may not be able to care for herself or her baby.

(Taylor, 2015, p 146)

B

Imagine looking at your newborn baby and being convinced they are the son of God. You may think this recent plotline in EastEnders sounds far-fetched. But it's actually a common symptom or post-partum psychosis, a condition that affects one in 500 mothers. "It's like being in a vivid nightmare only you don't wake up," says psychiatrist Dr Alain Gregoire, at the Winchester Mother and Baby Unit.

(Bates, 2016)

C

Postpartum psychosis (PP) is a serious, but rare, diagnosis occurring in around one in 1000 births. You're likely to experience a mix of:

- depression
- mania
- psychosis

Symptoms usually start quite suddenly within a few weeks after giving birth. PP is sometimes called puerperal psychosis. Postpartum psychosis can be an overwhelming and frightening experience for you and your loved ones, and it's important to seek help as soon as possible. With the right support, most women fully recover.

(Mind, no date)

Discussion: identifying formal style

Text A is taken from an academic textbook. Text B is taken from an online magazine. Text C is from the Mind mental health charity website.

CROSS
REFERENCE

Chapter 2,
Coherent
texts and
arguments,
Developing
a coherent
argument and
expressing
criticality

CROSS
REFERENCE

Chapter 3,
Referring to
sources

- Text A is objective and impersonal, as its principal aim is to inform a scholarly reader. The language is formal and technical ('severe episode'; 'sudden onset'; 'present'). It uses cautious language to avoid overgeneralisation ('can present'; 'may have'; 'may not be able'). The factual content is supported by reference to academic sources, presented according to academic conventions.

- Text B is very personal and colourful, as one of its principal aims is to engage the attention of a general, non-expert reader and keep their interest. It contains popular cultural references (son of God; EastEnders). It has informal grammar and punctuation (starting a sentence with an imperative – 'Imagine'; starting a sentence with 'But'; the use of personal pronouns – 'your newborn baby', 'you may'; the use of contractions – 'it's'). It contains conversational language ('actually'). It uses a lot of direct quotation and a lot of in-text detail about the source of the information, but it is lacking formal academic references – there is no evidential support for the claim about the number of mothers affected (and the number it gives differs from the figure given by Mind).

- Text C is neither very formal nor very informal in tone. Its aim is to inform and educate the general public, so it is generally clear and accessible to a non-expert reader. The language is mostly neutral and factual, but it is also personal and conversational, addressing the reader as 'you', and using contractions ('it's', 'you're'). Most of the vocabulary is neutral, apart from 'around', which is slightly informal, and 'loved ones', which has an emotional overtone. These less formal features give it a softer, almost comforting tone, while the generally neutral and factual style invites trust. The text also differs from the academic text in that it does not provide any evidence for the figure it provides on the numbers affected.

The formal style that characterises Text A (and parts of C) will be discussed in this section, and there will be guidance on how to avoid some of the informal features in Text B (and parts of C).

Other characteristics of academic writing such as the use of cautious language to indicate stance, and the role of references are discussed in other chapters of this book.

Task

Word choice

Look at the words below. What do they have in common? What differentiates them?

> minor juvenile paediatric kid bairn brat
> suckling offspring infant child

Discussion: word choice

These are all words associated with children, but they differ in terms of style and common usage. Language style can be broadly categorised as follows:

FORMAL	NEUTRAL	INFORMAL
infant	child	kid

CROSS
REFERENCE

Appendix 1,
English
language
references

Formal language can include specialised or technical terms, for example, scientific words such as 'offspring', and legal words such as 'minor' and 'juvenile'. In nursing, the specialised term 'paediatric', relating to the management of conditions affecting children, is commonly used.

So context is everything, and the university context requires specific language use. The language of academic writing can be neutral or formal, and it often includes specialised or technical terms. You must be careful to avoid informal, colloquial language like 'kid', including dialect words like 'bairn' (used in Scotland and some areas of Northern England), and slang words, especially those with derogatory associations, such as 'brat'. You should also be careful with some formal words, particularly those which are quite literary in nature. For example, the word 'suckling' can be used to describe a baby who has not yet been weaned, a concept familiar to nurses and midwives, but this is the kind of word you would expect to find in Shakespeare rather than an academic paper or medical notes. Dictionaries often provide information on the special characteristics of words.

Top tips

CROSS REFERENCE

Appendix 1, English language references

Using a thesaurus

A thesaurus can be a useful tool, but like any tool, it requires careful use. You should avoid unthinking reliance on the information it provides: the terms listed in a thesaurus as synonyms are often not exact synonyms, and there is often a lack of information on the style or usage of the term. For example, a thesaurus may provide the following synonyms for the word 'old':

elderly geriatric senile aged ancient decrepit venerable hoary over the hill

CROSS REFERENCE

Chapter 2, Coherent texts and arguments, Referring back in the text: repetition, variation and pronoun use

However, only the first three are appropriate for academic use, and even they have very specific uses: 'elderly' is more polite than 'old'; 'geriatric' is a technical term common in medical use; 'senile' can refer to the loss of mental faculties (though it can also be used in an insulting way in everyday slang). The other words would sound inappropriate, strange or disturbing in an academic essay or medical notes!

Before you use a word you have never used before, check in a good dictionary to find out information on usage and to see authentic examples containing the word. And remember that a synonym may not be the best choice; repeating the same word may help the reader more.

Also, note that some terms used in a healthcare environment may not even feature in a general thesaurus, for example, the term 'later life', which is a positive term commonly used by nurses in relation to elderly people.

Training in later life care is available to staff.

Gentle exercise can facilitate mobility in later life.

It is clear that some words should be avoided completely. However, a lot of language use is a matter of choice. You can often choose between a neutral word and a more formal word. Both will often be acceptable in an academic essay, but the more formal choice may well enhance your writing.

Task

Identifying inappropriate language

 Cross out the terms in the lists below which would be inappropriate in an academic essay because they are too informal or literary. It may be necessary to consult a dictionary for one or two of the words.

1) male/man/bloke

2) inebriated/tipsy/drunk

3) impecunious/poor/broke

4) food/nutrition/grub

5) sleep/slumber/doze

Task

Identifying formal language

Identify the more formal choice in the sentences below.

1) <u>Not much/Little</u> research has been carried out on the topic of perceived nursing needs of elderly patients during hospitalisation.

2) The patient's condition <u>deteriorated/got worse</u> overnight.

3) In 1991, Mary Seacole <u>got/was awarded</u> the Jamaican Order of Merit for her services to nursing.

4) There are <u>about/approximately</u> thirty patients on the ward.

5) Nurses are required to <u>adhere/keep</u> to the ethical principles <u>enshrined within/contained in</u> the NMC Code.

6) Nurses should <u>show/demonstrate</u> a capacity for empathy.

7) It is important to <u>ensure/make sure</u> that the patient is hydrated.

8) The patient was prescribed light exercise <u>such as/like</u> walking and swimming.

9) Nutritional standards in hospitals need to <u>get better/improve</u>.

10) A range of therapies can be employed to relieve pain and <u>facilitate/help</u> the healing process.

11) <u>More and more/An increasing number of</u> hospitals are offering outpatient care for this condition.

12) There are <u>a lot of/many</u> studies on palliative care.

Strategies for making your writing more formal

1) Avoid conversational expressions such as 'actually', 'by the way' or 'to be honest'.

2) Use the formal negatives, 'little/few', rather than the more conversational 'not much/not many':

  little time/energy/food (uncountable nouns)

  few patients/beds/experts (countable nouns)

3) It is grammatically correct to start a sentence with 'and' or 'but', and you will find sentences like this in academic texts. However, if you start too many sentences with these words, your style will seem too chatty and unstructured, so make good use of more formal options such as 'in addition' and 'however'.

4) Place adverbs before the main verb (rather than at the beginning or the end of a sentence, as is common in spoken English):

  Originally, the online asthma intervention programme was developed for school nurses.

  → The online asthma intervention programme was originally developed for school nurses.

5) Academic discourse aims to be objective. For this reason, care should be taken with the use of personalised language, including personal pronouns such as 'I/you/we'. There may be some situations in which you are expected to write in a personal style, for example, in a reflective essay, where you are required to discuss your thought processes etc; also, some academic journals, in medicine and psychology for example, have made the conscious decision to adopt a more direct style (eg the use of 'we', as in sentences such as 'We selected fifty samples', instead of passive constructions like 'Fifty samples were selected'). It is therefore necessary to consider each situation in isolation before making a choice about the type of language required. As far as academic assignments are concerned, most will require you to use impersonal structures such as those below:

  You can see a comparison of patient outcomes in Table 2.

  → A comparison of patient outcomes can be seen in Table 2.

  I think this approach is preferable.

  → There is evidence to support this approach (Cross, 2011; Turner, 2015).

6) Avoid contractions like 'they're', 'he's' and 'can't'. You will find contractions in many academic textbooks (occasionally in this one), as the writers want to make them accessible, but they are not felt to be appropriate in academic essays or scholarly journals.

7) Be cautious with informal punctuation such as dashes (–) and exclamation marks (!). Dashes are sometimes used as a type of parenthesis (as an alternative to brackets), but colons can often provide a more formal alternative:

> The problems faced by many rural facilities – a lack of trained midwives, basic equipment and supplies, and the physical distance between health centres and the areas they serve – are covered in the report.
>
> → The report covers the problems faced by many rural facilities: a lack of trained midwives, basic equipment and supplies, and the physical distance between health centres and the areas they serve.

CROSS REFERENCE

Colons

Task

Improving style

Rewrite the text below so that it is more formal and academic in style.

The aging population means that more and more people have to be carers and a lot of them are struggling. They often don't get help and they're facing cuts in the benefits and services they can get. We can see from lots of studies that the general health of carers gets worse the more hours of care they give. A great partnership with professionals will make outcomes for both carers and patients much better. All professionals – doctors, district nurses, general practice nurses – should respect carers as expert partners in care. And community nurses need to have certain values and skills – eg compassion, competence, commitment – to make sure carers' health and well-being is looked after.

Top tips

Using the Academic Word List

The **Academic Word List** (Coxhead, 2000) is a list of words which have a high frequency in English-language academic texts. The words at the top end of the list, ie the most frequent, include:

> analyse approach area assume benefit concept consistent context data established evidence factor identified indicate involved issue major method occur procedure process role significant specific theory variable

You can check if a word you want to use is on the list at: www.victoria.ac.nz/lals/resources/academicwordlist/

Grammar, spelling and punctuation

CROSS REFERENCE

Communication Skills

When lecturers read and assess your work, they are not looking for perfection. They will overlook occasional minor errors, as long as they do not interfere with the readability of the text or obscure the meaning. However, it is very hard to get high marks if there are numerous grammar, spelling or punctuation errors in your writing, even if the content is good. The standard of your English also has implications for professional practice: The NMC Code demands that you *'keep clear and accurate records relevant to your practice'* (2015, p 9), and this requires an awareness of good grammar, spelling and punctuation.

CROSS
REFERENCE

Appendix 2,
Grammatical
terminology

English grammar, spelling and punctuation can be a challenge both for students whose first language is not English and for some native speakers. In the UK, educational attitudes towards the explicit teaching of grammar to school children have varied greatly over the last few decades. Whatever the rights and wrongs of this, one of the outcomes is that some people in the UK may have learned very little about grammar at school. And even those who did may feel a bit hazy about some of the rules and terminology. In order to meet the standards necessary for academic success, it is necessary to grasp certain grammatical concepts. This section provides explanations and examples which will help students who lack confidence in this area. You will find more detailed explanations and examples of grammatical terms used in this chapter (in **bold** in the text) in Appendix 2.

CROSS
REFERENCE

Chapter 5,
Preparing
your work for
submission,
Editing and
proofreading
your final text

Sometimes, errors are down to insufficient proofreading, rather than a lack of knowledge. It is essential that you leave yourself enough time to read through your finished essay or report several times, firstly to make sure that it is readable and makes sense, and secondly to proofread and pick up 'typos' (typing errors), grammar, spelling and punctuation slips, or messy formatting.

Common areas of difficulty in grammar and spelling

There are a number of areas of grammar and spelling that cause particular problems.

Quantifiers

Quantifiers are words used before **nouns** (terms used for people, places or things) to indicate number or amount.

- The quantifier 'fewer' is used with **countable nouns** (literally things which can be counted, usually ending in 's' in English):

    less midwives/patients/beds ✗

    fewer midwives/patients/beds ✓

- The quantifier 'less' is used with **uncountable nouns** (things seen as a mass which cannot be split or counted):

    less pain/time/energy/sugar

- The quantifier 'amount' should only be used with uncountable nouns:

    a large amount of pregnant women ✗

    a large number of pregnant women ✓

    a large amount of bleeding ✓

Grammatical agreement

- Most **sentences** in English contain a **main clause** which is built upon two basic elements: a **subject**, and a **verb** which agrees with it:

    The treatment [subject] was [verb] successful.

    Many of the hospitals mentioned in the select committee's report [subject] are situated [verb] in densely populated urban areas.

    Be careful to make sure a verb agrees with its subject; it is quite easy to get this wrong if the main word in the subject and the verb are far apart, and if there are other nouns between the subject and verb:

    One of the most difficult challenges faced by nurses working shifts are maintaining work–life balance. ✗

    One of the most difficult challenges faced by nurses working shifts is maintaining work–life balance. ✓

- **Nouns** can sometimes be replaced with **pronouns** (short words such as 'he/it/them'). These pronouns must also agree with the noun they refer to:

    Information is supplied on the drugs and on how it is administered. ✗

    Information is supplied on the drugs and on how they are administered. ✓

The pens are preloaded with very short-acting <u>insulins</u>. <u>This</u> is injected after meals. ✗

The pens are preloaded with very short-acting <u>insulins</u>. <u>These</u> are injected after meals. ✓

CROSS
REFERENCE

Chapter 2,
Coherent
texts and
arguments,
Referring
back in the
text: repetition,
variation and
pronoun use

Commonly confused words

Many errors in students' written work arise because of confusion between certain words.

- Be careful to distinguish between 'there' and 'their'. The former introduces the theme of the sentence, or signifies place; the latter denotes possession:

    <u>There</u> are a number of issues affecting patients at this hospital.

    Carers have to be aware of <u>their</u> own needs too.

- Do not confuse 'effect' (noun) and 'affect' (verb):

    Nursing workload can have a profound <u>effect</u> on both nurses and their patients.

    Nursing workload can <u>affect</u> both nurses and their patients profoundly.

    There is a verb 'effect', but it has another meaning (to make happen, bring about), and is usually restricted to particular nouns such as 'change':

    A number of midwives reported that they felt powerless to <u>effect</u> change in their institutions.

- Be careful to distinguish between **singular** and **plural** with the following words:

    a recent <u>phenomenon</u> (singular)

    the study of several <u>phenomena</u> important to nursing (plural)

    provide evidence of practice related to each <u>criterion</u> (singular)

    meet all the <u>criteria</u> (plural)

- Differentiate between the following **noun** and **verb** spellings:

NOUN –*ice*	VERB –*ise*
advice	advise
device	devise
practice	practise
licence	license

Task

Commonly confused words

Choose the correct form of the word in the sentences below.

1) New government policy has implications for nursing <u>practice/practise</u>.

2) The policy affects the ability of midwives to <u>practice/practise</u> safely and effectively.

3) Patients were offered <u>advice/advise</u> on nutrition.

4) Midwives can <u>advice/advise</u> on preparation for home births.

5) A breast pump is a <u>device/devise</u> for drawing milk from a nursing mother's breasts.

6) The medical guidelines have been <u>deviced/devised</u> by the UN.

7) Midwives are <u>licenced/licensed</u> to administer medication.

8) Applicants must possess a valid driving <u>licence/license</u>.

9) The paper reported on the <u>affects/effects</u> of the drug.

10) A number of children were <u>affected/effected</u> by the virus.

11) The patients had followed <u>there/their</u> nutrition plans for six months.

12) <u>There/Their</u> is no known cure for the common cold.

Note that US English uses 'practice' and 'license' for both noun and verb.

Common areas of difficulty in punctuation

There are some strict rules governing punctuation in English; these rules are largely tied up with English grammar rules, such as the use of commas with relative clauses (discussed later in this section). However, in other cases, there are choices available to you; these choices are a question of style, but they are still important as they can affect clarity and readability. Some important punctuation rules and choices are discussed below.

The apostrophe

If you have problems with apostrophes, you are not alone! David Crystal, a well-known linguistics scholar, cites apostrophe use as one of the most problematic aspects of the English language: '*Another day when the phone doesn't stop ringing, and (once again) all because of the apostrophe*' (Crystal, 2012). It is a topic which clearly exercises the general British public, judging by the number of letters sent to newspapers to complain of apostrophe misuse! However, there are some simple rules which can help.

- After a **singular noun**, or a **proper noun** (like a name), **'s** is used to denote possession:

    in this patient's best interests

    Theresa May's policy on the NHS

    After **plural nouns**, and **proper nouns** ending in **s**, the apostrophe comes after the **s**:

    in these patients' best interests

    Burns' book, *Adult Nursing*

    It is also acceptable to add a possessive **s** in this case, as in 'Burns's book', but be consistent. Be careful with irregular plurals not ending in s – the apostrophe comes before the possessive **s**.

    the children's parents

- Apostrophes also signal missing letters in **contractions** like 'can't' (cannot), 'doesn't' (does not) and 'they'll' (they will).

    Do not confuse words which sound the same but have different meanings, grammar and spelling:

    - 'it's' is the contracted form of 'it is/has', whereas 'its' is a **possessive pronoun** like 'my' or 'her':

        The hospital provided details of <u>its</u> policy on staff development.

        <u>It's</u> hot today.

    - 'your' is a possessive pronoun, while 'you're' is a contraction of 'you are'.

        Always wash <u>your</u> hands.

        <u>You're</u> late.

    - 'they're' is a contraction of 'they are', distinct from 'there' and 'their'

        <u>There</u> is pressure on hospitals to stay within <u>their</u> budgets.

        <u>They're</u> here!

    You will avoid this problem if you write, as you should, without using contractions.

Hyphens

Multi-word **adjectives** (words which describe nouns), such as the first word of this sentence, are usually hyphenated when they come before a noun, but not when they come after:

- an out-of-date nursing practice
- a nursing practice which is out of date
- a three-day-old baby
- a baby who is three days old

Brackets

Brackets should be used sparingly as they can interrupt the flow of a text. If you do use them, be aware of the rules.

- If the bracketed information is part of the sentence, it requires no specific punctuation:

    The data (collected over a three-month period) revealed a significant improvement in mobility.

    The brackets here could be replaced with commas or perhaps dashes (though dashes are a little on the informal side).

- If the brackets contain a separate sentence, it should be punctuated as such:

    The data revealed a significant improvement in mobility. (The data was collected over a three-month period.) Several patients noted improved joint movement.

    In cases like this, brackets are just one choice available for reducing the focus on this piece of information. Other choices include:

    The data, which was collected over a three-month period, revealed a significant improvement in mobility.

Punctuation and sentence structure

The use of full stops, commas, colons and semi-colons is intrinsically linked with the control of sentence structure in English. Some of the most important rules and patterns are detailed below. Most example sentences in this section are authentic examples from academic nursing textbooks (Burns, 2015; Pryjmachuk, 2011a).

Full stops

Full stops are the most straightforward of punctuation marks and they do not really cause problems for students (although their misuse is linked with 'fragments' and 'run-ons', discussed later in this section). Suffice it to say that they are the main way of indicating the boundaries between **sentences**.

A patient will usually be admitted to an intensive care unit after surgery. Here, they can be monitored by specialist nursing staff.

Commas

Commas are the equivalent of changing gear when driving; you come to a point where you need to slow down a little or turn a corner. The commas help you negotiate these changes, but also, and perhaps more importantly, they enable you to take your reader along with you.

(Peck and Coyle, 2012, p 54)

So commas can be a way of guiding, or 'driving', your reader through the text. Below are some common patterns in comma use.

- It can make a sentence easier to read if the parts of a **sentence** which come before, after, or in the middle of the main idea are separated with commas, especially in longer sentences:

    According to the World Health Organisation (2011), non-communicable diseases are the leading causes of death globally.

    (Ormrod and Burns, 2015, p 278)

As an adult nurse, you will be responsible and accountable for keeping your own knowledge and skills up to date through continuing professional development and lifelong learning.

(Gregory, 2015, p 102)

All patients, regardless of the setting, have the potential to become acutely and critically unwell.

(Tierney et al, 2015, p 313)

Postpartum (or puerperal) psychosis is a severe episode of mental illness representing a psychiatric emergency, with a sudden onset during the days or weeks following childbirth.

(Taylor, 2015, p 146)

These commas are not obligatory, and some people prefer not to use them too much as they believe they 'clutter up' the text. When you have a choice like this, let it be motivated by sensitivity to the experience of the reader. Will a comma help the reader navigate the text more easily and focus on the most important information in the sentence?

- It is not obligatory to use a comma before 'and/but/or' when using them to join words or parts of a sentence, but it can often help to make long sentences easier to read. Again, be sensitive to the experience of the reader. In the first example below, the comma before 'but' helps break up a complex sentence with many grammatical elements into two discernible ideas; in the second example, commas signal the three items in the list introduced by the colon ('giving', 'managing', 'involving'), the second 'and' thus clearly forming part of the third item:

Traditionally, care of the older person has been seen as a less attractive career pathway in comparison to other specialist areas of adult nursing, but in reality it is a rewarding and challenging field of nursing that is ripe for further development and innovation.

(Stanmore and Brown Wilson, 2015, p 365)

As an adult nurse, you will need to be proactive in involving older people in their care decisions from the onset: giving explanations, managing expectations, and involving families in decision making and discharge planning.

(Stanmore and Brown Wilson, 2015, p 370)

- The **main clause** (the main idea in a sentence) in a **sentence** is usually separated with a comma from a **participle clause** (an '–ing' or '–ed' verb form adding information). This comma is not obligatory, but it can help the reader to follow a long sentence:

All nurses must work effectively across professional and agency boundaries, actively involving and respecting the contribution of others to the provision of person-centred care.

(Rogers, 2015, p 63)

- Another clause can also be added to a **main clause** with a linking **conjunction** such as 'although/because/whilst'. These two parts of the sentence can be separated with a comma, especially when the main clause follows the other clause:

Whilst cerebrovascular disease tends to affect adults, children can also be affected.

(Ormrod and Burns, 2015, p 279)

- Commas are not used before **that-clauses** (structures following certain verbs etc):

Wale et al. (2007) recognise, that the skill of airway management is important for any healthcare provider caring for critically ill patients. ✘
Wale et al. (2007) recognise that the skill of airway management is important for any healthcare provider caring for critically ill patients. ✔

(Tierney et al, 2015, p 328)

- Do not use commas directly in between a **subject** and **verb**, no matter how long the subject:

> The assessment of a person's capacity to give or withhold consent, is considered in relation to a specific decision. ✘
> The assessment of a person's capacity to give or withhold consent is considered in relation to a specific decision. ✓
>
> (Tierney et al, 2015, p 345)

Task

Variation in comma use

The two texts below are well written and do not break any punctuation rules. However, they differ in their use of commas. This may be due to individual choice, or editorial policy (they are both from textbooks).

 What differences in comma use can you find? Which style do you prefer? Why?

A

The assessment of a person's capacity to give or withhold consent is considered in relation to a specific decision. While the individual may not have capacity to make some decisions they may still retain capacity for other decisions. For example a patient may not have capacity to make a decision regarding a surgical procedure but could retain capacity to consent (or not) to having their clinical observations (e.g. blood pressure) checked.

(Tierney et al, 2015, p 345)

B

As far as individual nursing practice is concerned, mental health nurses more often than not adopt the perspective(s) that most appeal to them. However, given the current emphasis on evidence-based practice, it is important that we do not let ideological dogma alone dominate our practice. Though there are some practitioners who rigidly adhere to one or other of the theoretical frameworks, these are the exception rather than the rule. Most skilled practitioners take an eclectic approach: they have an awareness of the strengths and weaknesses of the various perspectives and models, and they use their professional judgement to select a treatment approach most suitable for a given set of circumstances.

(Pryjmachuk, 2011b, p 36)

Colons

Colons are used to introduce something that expands in some way on what precedes it, by, for example, providing an explanation, or listing items:

> The medical model dominates the delivery and organisation of physical healthcare: medical specialities in most hospitals reflect the physiological systems of the body.
>
> (Pryjmachuk, 2011b, p 13)

Semi-colons

A semi-colon can be used instead of a full stop to separate **sentences** which are closely connected.

CROSS REFERENCE

Parallel structures

CROSS
REFERENCE

Parallel
structures

Decision making in healthcare ethics is usually concerned with eliciting good outcomes; values-based practice, on the other hand, is more concerned with the decision making process than specific outcomes.

(Pryjmachuk, 2011c, p 57)

Focus on fragments and run-on sentences

It has been established that most **sentences** in English contain a **main clause** which contains two basic elements: a **subject** and a **verb** which agrees with it:

Nursing [subject] is [verb] a profession within the health care sector.

School nurses [subject] are [verb] vital to their schools and communities.

If a sentence is lacking a main clause, or if a main clause is lacking a subject or a main verb, the sentence is incomplete, ie it is a 'fragment':

While the majority reported only mild anxiety. ✘ (no main clause)

While the majority reported only mild anxiety, a small number were seriously affected. ✓

Nursing integration into schools and communities. ✘ (no verb)

Nurses have been integrated into schools and communities. ✓

Lately, have admitted patients in large numbers. ✘ (no subject)

Lately, rural clinics have admitted patients in large numbers. ✓

If there is more than one subject/verb structure, they should be separated by full stops or semi-colons, or connected (with **conjunctions**, for example). If only a comma is used, it creates a 'run-on sentence', which is grammatically incorrect:

School nurses are integrated into their schools and communities, they provide vital health care information. ✘

School nurses are integrated into their schools and communities; they provide vital health care information. ✓

School nurses are integrated into their schools and communities, and they provide vital health care information. ✓

Run-on sentences also include those beginning with words and phrases used to connect two sentences such as 'however/therefore/as a result':

Psychology is a central part of undergraduate nursing curricula in the UK, however, student nurses report difficulties recognising its relevance and value. ✘

Psychology is a central part of undergraduate nursing curricula in the UK. However, student nurses report difficulties recognising its relevance and value. ✓

Psychology is a central part of undergraduate nursing curricula in the UK; however, student nurses report difficulties recognising its relevance and value. ✓

Focus on 'hanging participles'

As discussed above, it is common to attach a **participle clause** to a main clause. However, it is important to make sure that the two parts of such a sentence are clearly connected.

Being prone to infection, nurses are required to take precautions with these patients. ✘

Being prone to infection, these patients require special precautions. ✓

Admitted with a history of psychosis, a psychiatric nurse examined the patient. ✘

Admitted with a history of psychosis, the patient was examined by a psychiatric nurse. ✓

In the examples marked as incorrect, it is as if the nurses are being described by the first clause. This can also happen with other phrases, creating a certain ambiguity in the example below.

Without an understanding of what their treatment entails, nurses cannot empower patients to make informed decisions. ✗

Without an understanding of what their treatment entails, patients cannot be empowered to make informed decisions. ✓

Focus on relative clauses

The pronouns 'that' and 'which' are used to refer back to nouns in what are called 'relative clauses'. These are very common in academic writing because they are very useful for defining terms and adding information to the main topic of a sentence. However, the rules are quite complicated and mistakes are quite common. In brief, 'that' and 'which' can both be used to refer back to something which is being defined or restricted in some way (restrictive/defining relative clauses); 'that' or 'who' are used for people. There are no commas in this case:

Forceps are a device that/which can be used to hurry delivery when the mother or baby is in distress during labour. (defining; one type of device)

Specialised knowledge is required for nurses who/that are responsible for treating terminally ill patients. (restricted subset of nurses)

Only 'which' (or 'who' for people) can be used when extra adding information (non-restrictive/non-defining relative clauses) which relates to the whole group or idea, not a subset. This type of clause can be removed from the sentence without making the sentence ungrammatical. Commas must be used in these sentences:

Patients are encouraged to set both short-term and long-term goals, which can often facilitate recovery.

One type of psychotherapy is cognitive behavioural therapy (CBT), which is used to treat a wide variety of psychological disorders.

Nurses, who treat many victims of violent crime, are uniquely placed to contribute to education on this issue.

Refining grammar and punctuation

Task

Grammar and punctuation

1) Punctuate the text below so that it makes sense.

social factors also seem to influence depression rates depression is more common in the unemployed those living alone those who are divorced or separated those living in local authority or housing association accommodation those with a lower socioeconomic status and or material disadvantage and those with no formal educational qualifications social factors such as isolation racist attacks and dissatisfaction with housing may also contribute to depression in refugee groups indeed in traumatised refugees and asylum seekers poor social support seems to be a stronger predictor of depression in the long term than the severity of the initial trauma.

(Adapted from Briddon et al, 2011, p 108)

2) Correct the grammar and punctuation mistakes in the text below.

Postnatal depression effects 10–15 in every 100 woman after childbirth. It can be difficult to detect because it may present different in different women. The symptoms of postnatal depression is similar to that of depression at any other stage of life, the difference is the presence of a baby, that is likely to be the focus of the womans thoughts and difficulties. The disorder maybe mild or severe. Milder forms might be treat within the primary healthcare team. While more severe forms will require additional input from psychiatric services. Diagnosing postnatal depression requires clinical assessment by GP or mental health specialist, however, nursing and midwifery staff, must be alert to the disorder in order make timely referrals.

(Adapted from Taylor, 2015, p 145)

Top tips

Spelling and grammar check

Use a spell and grammar tool, but always double-check that the suggestion given to you makes sense, as these computer programmes cannot recognise some subtleties of usage, especially in grammar. Also, make sure your spell and grammar check is set to UK English, as there are a number of differences between UK and US English, and it is important to be consistent.

	UK	US
–ise v *–ize*	prioritise, recognise	prioritize, recognize*
–our v *–or*	colour, behaviour	color; behavior
–re v *–er*	centre, metre	center, meter
–ll– v *–l–*	travelling, cancelled	traveling, canceled

*The 'z' spelling is also acceptable in UK English; just be consistent.

Parallel structures

Parallel structures are formed when there is repetition of words, phrases, grammatical structures and punctuation patterns (combined with contrasting elements which move the text forward). They are common in academic writing because they are useful tools for organising information clearly, particularly when comparing and contrasting, or when listing items; Note how these structures often include colons and semi-colons as organisational tools, eg:

Schön (1983) distinguishes between <u>reflection on action</u> and <u>reflection in action</u>. <u>Reflecting on action</u> happens <u>after the event</u>, <u>reflection in action</u> <u>during the event</u>. <u>Reflection on action is</u> a prerequisite to becoming <u>a competent practitioner</u>; <u>reflection in action</u>, on the other hand, <u>is</u> a deeper skill that is essential if you are to become <u>a capable practitioner</u>.

(Pryjmachuk, 2011c, p 67)

There are many reasons for an error in administering medication. Two common types are: *procedural error* (e.g. <u>failing</u> to check the patient's identity) and *clinical error* (e.g. <u>administering</u> the wrong drug or dose).

(Gregory, 2015, p 95)

Physical medicine has made significant progress in dealing with the consequences of trauma, illness and disease: <u>it has cured</u> people of terrible diseases such as small pox; <u>it has enabled</u> people to survive following traumatic injuries; and, through transplantation, <u>it has extended</u> the lives of those with failing organs.

(Pryjmachuk, 2011b, p 12)

Notice how the *repetition* of certain phrases and structures highlights the information which is *different*, eg 'on' vs 'in'; 'capable' vs 'competent'; 'procedural' vs 'clinical'. This combination of repetition and change makes the text very easy to process for the reader (McIntyre, 1997).

Be careful to avoid 'faulty parallelism', ie when items in a list do not share the same grammar:

Physical medicine has made significant progress in dealing with the consequences of trauma, illness and disease: <u>it has cured</u> people of terrible diseases such as small pox; <u>enabling</u> people to survive following traumatic injuries; and, through transplantation, <u>extension</u> of the lives of those with failing organs. ✗

Task

Parallel structures

Use the notes below to write short texts using parallel structures. Think about how you might use commas, colons and semi-colons to organise the information.

1) medication errors – impact – patient/nurse/organisation

2) initiative – Family Nurse Partnership Programme (FNP) – help young, vulnerable first-time mothers – aims – improve pregnancy outcomes/child health and development/ parents' economic self-sufficiency

3) some elderly patients – mobile, eg driving, playing golf/others – largely sedentary, eg spending a lot of time indoors reading/watching TV

4) three main theories underpin decision-making process in nursing (Standing, 2010) – normative, descriptive, prescriptive

Summary

This chapter has analysed elements of academic style and provided strategies to help you write clear, accurate English for academic purposes. It has outlined the choices available to you in terms of expression, grammatical structures and punctuation, as you complete your written assignments. In addition, it has outlined some of the most challenging areas of English grammar and punctuation, in order to help you avoid common errors and refine your writing. Good style and accuracy will help you to create a good impression in your writing, and allow your ideas to shine through.

Sources of example texts

Bates, C (2016) 'I Was Convinced that my Baby Would Die the Next Day'. *BBC News Magazine*, 16th February [online]. Available at: www.bbc.co.uk/news/magazine-35543747 (accessed 13 May 2017).

Briddon, J, Baguley, C and Rolfe, L (2011) Helping People Recover from Depression. In Pryjmachuk, S (ed) *Mental Health Nursing: An Evidence-Based Introduction*. London: Sage, 105–46.

Burns, D (ed) (2015) *Foundations of Adult Nursing*. London: Sage.

Gregory, J (2015) Medicines Management. In Burns, D (ed) *Foundations of Adult Nursing*. London: Sage, 89–108.

Ormrod, J and Burns, D (2015) Supportive Care: Caring for Adults with Long-term Conditions. In Burns, D (ed) *Foundations of Adult Nursing*. London: Sage, 275–312.

Mind (no date). Postnatal Depression and Perinatal Mental Health [online]. Available at: www.mind.org.uk/information-support/types-of-mental-health-problems/postnatal-depression-and-perinatal-mental-health/postpartum-psychosis/#.WJdNp_mLTIU (accessed 13 May 2017).

Pryjmachuk, S (ed) (2011a) *Mental Health Nursing: An Evidence-based Introduction*. London: Sage.

Pryjmachuk, S (2011b) Theoretical Perspectives in Mental Health Nursing. In Pryjmachuk, S (ed) *Mental Health Nursing: An Evidence-Based Introduction*. London: Sage, 3–41.

Pryjmachuk, S (2011c) The Capable Mental Health Nurse. In Pryjmachuk, S (ed) *Mental Health Nursing: An Evidence-Based Introduction*. London: Sage, 42–72.

Rogers, J (2015) Interprofessional and Multidisciplinary Team Working. In Burns, D (ed) *Foundations of Adult Nursing*. London: Sage, 63–88.

Stanmore, E and Brown Wilson, C (2015) Caring for the Older Person. In Burns, D (ed) *Foundations of Adult Nursing*. London: Sage, 361–94.

Taylor, G (2015) Exposure to Other Fields of Nursing. In Burns, D (ed) *Foundations of Adult Nursing*. London: Sage, 135–78.

Tierney, P, Freeman, S and Gregory, J (2015) Caring for the Acutely Ill Adult. In Burns, D (ed) *Foundations of Adult Nursing*. London: Sage, 313–60.

References

Academic Word List. [online] Available at: www.victoria.ac.nz/lals/resources/academicwordlist (accessed 2 April 2017).

Coxhead, A (2000) A New Academic Wordlist. *TESOL Quarterly*, 34, 213–38.

Crystal, D (2012) On Waterstone(')s. *DCBLOG* [online]. Available at: http://david-crystal.blogspot.co.uk/2012/01/on-waterstones.html (accessed 2 April 2017).

McIntyre, M (1997) Lucidity and Science I: Writing Skills and the Pattern Perception Hypothesis. *Interdisciplinary Science Reviews*, 22, 199–216.

Nursing and Midwifery Council (2015). *The Code: Professional Standards of Practice and Behaviour for Nurses and Midwives* [online]. Available at: www.nmc.org.uk/globalassets/sitedocuments/nmc-publications/nmc-code.pdf (accessed 13 May 2017).

Peck, J and Coyle, M (2012) *Write it Right: The Secrets of Effective Writing*. 2nd ed. New York: Palgrave Macmillan.

Chapter 5
Preparing your work for submission

Learning outcomes

After reading this chapter you will:

- know how to check that the work you submit meets university requirements;
- understand how to edit and proofread your work before submission, and be aware of some of the issues related to this process;
- be able to format and present your work to a high professional standard;
- be aware of some of the writing support available to you at university.

This chapter will help you to assess if a piece of work is ready to be submitted. It offers advice on the final edit of your text, including proofreading. It provides you with information and guidance on formatting and presentation. It also presents the options available to you if you feel you need further professional support with your writing.

Are you ready to submit your work?

When lecturers mark your work, they refer very closely to assessment guidelines and marking descriptors. It is therefore very important that you pay equally close attention to these documents. You should use these as the starting point for your assessment, and as a kind of 'checklist' at the end of the writing process, before you submit. The next section covers some of the most important considerations when preparing your work for submission.

Have you done what you were asked to do?

Checklist

- Have you answered the question or responded to the task in a direct, comprehensive and appropriate way?
- Is the content relevant?
- Have you supported your points and ideas with credible sources and evidence?
- Is your referencing complete, accurate and consistent?
- Have you followed all the guidelines on content, referencing, formatting and presentation to the letter?

Have you stuck to the word count?

You will most certainly be penalised if you either *fail to meet* or *exceed* the specified word count. Word counts are not arbitrary numbers plucked out of the air. They are decided on with a range of factors in mind.

- Word counts ensure equity since all students are given the same limit.
- Written assignments need to be a certain length in order to allow for the inclusion of a substantial amount of detail and/or a substantive argument.
- Word counts can be used to differentiate between different levels of study: for example, a third-year student should be expected to produce more writing on a given topic than a first-year student.
- Word limits require students to be selective in their response to a task, demonstrating their judgement regarding the most important aspects of a topic.

- Word limits require students to avoid redundancy (repetition of information or unnecessary repetition of words).
- Word limits require students to write concisely, to avoid 'wordiness'.

Most universities allow you a 10 per cent leeway either side (this is what 'plus or minus 10 per cent' means), so a 2,500 word assignment needs to be between 2,250 (2,500 – 250) and 2,750 (2,500 + 250) words. One side of A4, typed in a standard font (say Arial 12pt) and using double line spacing, normally contains between 250 and 300 words; so you can get a rough idea of how many words you have got by multiplying the number of pages by this figure. For example, if you have typed 11 pages, you will have around 2,750–3,300 words in total. The word count usually excludes your reference list, but double-check with the module leader if this is not mentioned in the assessment guidelines.

Are you clear about the submission process?

Checklist

- Are you required to submit a hard copy or to upload your document via your VLE? (You may need to do both.)
- If submitting a hard copy, how many copies do you need to submit, and in what form (eg A4, printed on one side or on both sides, secured in a folder or stapled)?
- Do you need to complete and attach a **standard cover sheet**? Or are you expected to create your own cover sheet? (You may be able to do both.)
- Where do you need to hand in hard copies (eg the school office, the office of a particular member of staff)?
- If submitting online, do you know the exact procedure? Make sure you find out about this in good time. Perhaps ask the module lecturer if it is possible to do a practice submission beforehand. (Many lecturers arrange an unassessed formative assignment and practice submission early in the course, so make sure you take advantage of such an opportunity.)
- Are you required to make your submission anonymous? (This is usually the case.) If so, have you been careful to make sure your name is not visible? Have you included your student number?
- Ensure you know the *exact* deadline for submission (including any personal deadlines or extensions you may have been given); electronic systems may deny a submission, or flag it up as late, at 4:01pm if the deadline is 4:00pm.

CROSS
REFERENCE

Presentation

Editing and proofreading your final text

Before you hand in the final version of your text, you need to read through it with two separate aims in mind. The first type of reading should be a type of **final editing**, where you focus on meaning and flow, making sure that everything hangs together and makes sense. The second type of reading is **proofreading**, where you check the text for surface errors in spelling, grammar and punctuation. This is also an opportunity to pick up on any problems with typing or formatting. Many students overlook the first type of reading (a final edit of content, organisation and meaning), and focus purely on looking for mistakes. However, it is important to do both. The two processes will obviously overlap: while reading to check meaning, you might also catch a few mistakes; while proofreading, you might encounter a possible ambiguity, for instance. This is to be expected, but you should take care not to be distracted from your principal aim.

Editing your final text

Make sure you leave enough time to read through your work several times to ensure that another person reading your essay will be able to follow what you have said and understand the points you want to make.

Top tips

CROSS
REFERENCE

Chapter 2,
Coherent
texts and
arguments,
Editing and
redrafting for
coherence

The final edit

- Reading out loud can help you put yourself in the reader's shoes and get a good sense of the flow and naturalness of the text.
- Trying to read the same text over and over is difficult to do, as your brain tends to switch off. Read it once, then put the text aside and go for a walk or make a cup of tea. You will come back to the text with fresh eyes.

Systematic treatment of names and titles

In nursing, you will often be required to refer to the names of medical conditions, such as 'malaria' or 'Parkinson's disease', and to the titles of professional organisations, such as the National Health Service or the Nursing and Midwifery Council. When referring to these, it is important to establish the conventions regarding the use of **capitalisation**.

- Most diseases and conditions are not capitalised, eg malaria, deep vein thrombosis, obsessive compulsive disorder.
- Diseases and conditions named after an individual capitalise the name, eg Parkinson's disease, Crohn's disease, Hodgkin's lymphoma.
- The titles of organisations are capitalised, eg the National Health Service.

Many conditions and organisations are also known by their **acronyms**. An acronym is the short form of a multi-word name, usually formed using the first letter of each word, eg:

- deep vein thrombosis (DVT);
- obsessive compulsive disorder (OCD);
- the National Health Service (NHS);
- the Nursing and Midwifery Council (NMC).

Often, people are more familiar with the acronym than the name, sometimes to the extent that they can be a little hazy on what it actually stands for!

In your writing, it is important to be systematic in your use of names and acronyms. The rule in academic writing is very simple: when you mention a term for the first time, you should use the full name, with the acronym following immediately in parentheses; after this, you should always use the acronym. The following example demonstrates this clearly.

> Lower extremity deep vein thrombosis (DVT) is the most frequent venous thromboembolism (VTE) observed in hospitalised patients (Nutescu, 2007). One of the important and well-known risk factors of DVT development is surgery. If there are additional risk factors in a patient undergoing a surgical operation, the risk of DVT is increased even further (Geerts et al. 2012).
>
> (Ayhan et al, 2015, p 2248)

CROSS
REFERENCE

Chapter 2,
Coherent
texts and
arguments

Systematic use of names and acronyms adds to the flow and coherence of the text.

Note that acronyms are different from **abbreviations**, which are formed by shortening a word, eg:

- approx (approximately);
- etc (from the Latin 'et cetera', meaning 'and so on').

The fact that something has been abbreviated is often indicated by the full stop at the end (approx., etc.), but this is often omitted (as in this book, for example). The important thing is to be consistent.

Systems for highlighting language

In academic writing, **bold**, *italics* and 'quotation marks' are often used to highlight text in some way. It is important that you are systematic and consistent in your use of these.

Task

Systems for highlighting language

What 'systems' for highlighting language are used by the writers below?

A

Rubella virus (RV) is the causative agent of a childhood disease commonly known as "German measles". RV is classified as the only member of the genus *Rubivirus* within the family *Togaviridae*. The latter is derived from the Latin "toga", meaning "cloak" or "shroud" (Lee and Boden, 2000).

B

Research into schizophrenia has often focused on the role of the family. In the 1950s, the focus appeared to be on the family's role in the *causation* of the disorder. Consider, for example, Lidz et al's notion of 'pathological' families (1965) and the 'double-bind' hypothesis of Bateson et al (1956).

C

Some behaviours that can enhance the therapeutic relationship use elements of both verbal and non-verbal communication. These include the skill of **active listening**. Active listening …

(Pryjmachuk, 2011, p 63)

Discussion: systems for highlighting language

- In A, the writer uses italics for Latin terms, and double quotation marks for highlighting words whose meaning is being discussed.
- In B, the writer uses italics for emphasis, and single quotation marks to quote terms from the literature. It is a good idea to reserve one type of quotation mark (single or double) for quotations only; this may be specified in your assessment guidelines, but, if not, just make sure you are consistent.
- In C, the writer uses bold for the first mention of a key term. This is very common in textbooks as it helps students to identify important concepts.

Proofreading

Proofreading is the final component of the writing process. It is the process whereby you check the text for surface errors in spelling, grammar and punctuation, and make sure that there are no typing mistakes ('typos') or formatting errors/inconsistencies.

Proofreading is actually a thorny issue. Firstly, students sometimes confuse it with the editing and redrafting process described in Chapter 2 (including the 'final edit' referred to above). In fact, proofreading should only involve the correction of small surface errors; it should not involve changing the meaning or structure of your work.

Secondly, proofreading can be something you do yourself, or it can be something you ask or employ someone else to do. There are no uniform guidelines across UK universities with respect to this process, so it is important that you consider the issues involved carefully. If you decide to employ a professional proofreader, you should first find out if your university offers a proofreading service. If no official services are available, you should seek recommendations from friends or fellow students. When you have made a decision, make sure that you and the proofreader make contact beforehand to discuss the terms of your 'contract'. You should both be very clear on what can be expected. The proofreader can be asked to clean up surface errors in spelling, grammar and punctuation, but they should not be involved in changing the structure or meaning of your work. There are good reasons for this: firstly, universities obviously expect work submitted by students to be their own work in essence (though they accept that students may ask for help with grammar and punctuation); secondly, you do not want your own voice or message to be distorted in any way.

Thirdly, be very clear that anyone who proofreads your work is merely *making suggestions*; it is then up to you to consider these, and to accept or reject them. Ultimately, only you are responsible for your work.

Top tips

Proofreading

- Become adept at proofreading your own writing by noting the kind of errors that have been picked up on in previous assignments, and focusing on these.

- Make use of the spelling and grammar check tool of your word processing program. Microsoft Word will indicate spelling mistakes by underlining them in red, and grammar mistakes by underlining them in green. (These will also help you identify some typing and formatting issues, eg, too many/no spaces between words.) This is a very useful tool, but it is to be treated with caution: it is a computer program, not a human being, and thus, sometimes cannot identify a particular nuance in a text. You need to assess each suggestion carefully.

- You should always be involved in proofreading your own work, but many people, including experienced academics, sometimes ask a peer or colleague to look at their writing. In this way, proofreading can become a type of collaborative activity, one that could enable you to develop a skill that will be essential in future academic studies and your work life. This is distinct from the academic malpractice of collusion, where a student takes credit for work they are not responsible for.

Task

Proofreading practice

 Find and correct errors of spelling, grammar, punctuation and formatting in the following texts.

A

Femail hormone are immplicated in a number of cancers.The contraceptive pill contains low dose of the hormone oestrogen which is linked with breast, cervical cancer, however they also contain progesterone which is know to be protective against endometrial cancer. According to the NHS, the risks associated with the pill, are relative small for most of women and it's benefits outweigh the risks. There are however a number of women who is more at risk, including those over 35, smokers, those with high blood pressure

B

Of central importance, to the cognitive psychologists is the 'schema' notion. A schema is a mental "template" that guides behaviour or thought, in a similar way that a recipe is a template for creating an exotic dish [schemata actually guide external and external action, external action being observable behaviour, internal action being thought]. Any action, internal or external, will have a schema underpinning it.

Thus, there are schemata for skilled tasks,like driving or typing, schemata for making judgements about people, schemata for language, schemata for perceiving, and so on. some aspect's of certain schemata may be inherited (indeed, the simplest schemata are mere reflex action's), the vast majority are acquired. To those familiar with Computers, a schema is little more than the software that drives our action. however, unlike Computer Software, schemata can replicate,change and become redundant as we experience the world.

Schemata, help us process the vast amount, of information in the world.they serve us well for the majority of the time; however, they are not always applicable to a particular situation and when we misapply them, error's occur, for example, when we misapply a "braking" schema whilst driving,we might be involved in an accident. Similarly,the misapplication of 'judgemental' schemata can lead to the creation of stereotypes.

Formatting

CROSS
REFERENCE

*Studying for
your Nursing
Degree*,
Chapter 6,
Assessment

In written assessments, you will be judged on the breadth of your knowledge, the depth of your understanding, the quality of your ideas and analysis, and the clarity and coherence of your writing. However, even the best work cannot fully impress the reader if it is poorly formatted and presented. Untidy presentation and inconsistent formatting will hinder the reader's ability to navigate your text. It can also suggest a 'sloppy' or unprofessional approach. It is for these reasons that formatting and presentation usually form part of the criteria for assessment in marking descriptors.

The following tasks will help you understand how seemingly minor formatting choices can greatly affect the reader. The subsequent discussions will guide you towards formatting and presenting your work clearly and professionally.

Line spacing

Task

Line spacing

Look at the three versions of work below. What differences do you notice in the formatting of the text? Which version is usually *not* acceptable in university work? Why?

A

Keyhole surgery is carried out by making a small incision in the skin. It can be used in the treatment of many conditions, such as cancer and Crohn's disease. In keyhole surgery, the wound is relatively small, and so leaves a smaller scar and causes less pain than traditional surgery. Patients treated with keyhole surgery usually recover quicker and are able to leave hospital sooner. As the technology advances, keyhole surgery is becoming increasingly common and it is used almost exclusively in some areas.

B

Keyhole surgery is carried out by making a small incision in the skin. It can be used in the treatment of many conditions, such as cancer and Crohn's disease. In keyhole surgery, the wound is relatively small, and so leaves a smaller scar and causes less pain than traditional surgery. Patients treated with keyhole surgery usually recover quicker and are able to leave hospital sooner. As the technology advances, keyhole surgery is becoming increasingly common and it is used almost exclusively in some areas.

C

Keyhole surgery is carried out by making a small incision in the skin. It can be used in the treatment of many conditions, such as cancer and Crohn's disease. In keyhole surgery, the wound is relatively small, and so leaves a smaller scar and causes less pain than traditional surgery. Patients treated with keyhole surgery usually recover quicker and are able to leave hospital sooner. As the technology advances, keyhole surgery is becoming increasingly common and it is used almost exclusively in some areas.

Discussion: line spacing

The three texts have been formatted with different line spacing. A is **single-spaced**, B is **1.5 spaced**, and C is **double-spaced**. (In Microsoft Word, line spacing is adjusted through the 'paragraph' tool on the toolbar.) Assessment guidelines usually specify the line spacing you should use. Most guidelines specify 1.5 or double spaced, for two reasons.

- Most people find single-spaced writing a bit difficult to read.
- The person assessing your work may wish to add comments or corrections directly onto the text, either on paper, or using VLE tools such as Feedback Studio (Blackboard) and this is not possible when the line spacing is too narrow.

Paragraph formatting

Task

Paragraph formatting

Look at the four versions of work below. What differences do you notice in the formatting of paragraphs? Which version is *not* acceptable? Why?

A

The family has played a central role in research into schizophrenia since the 1950s when, admittedly, the focus appeared to be on the family's role in the causation of the disorder. Consider, for example, Lidz et al's notion of 'pathological' families (1965) and the 'double-bind' hypothesis of Bateson et al (1956).
Around the same time as these 'causal' hypotheses were being promoted, the anti-psychotic drugs were discovered. Drugs, by their very nature, are treatments designated for the individual and this fact coupled with the prevailing view of families as toxic agents led, unsurprisingly, to what could cynically be called the first family intervention strategy – that of excluding the family.

B

The family has played a central role in research into schizophrenia since the 1950s when, admittedly, the focus appeared to be on the family's role in the causation of the disorder. Consider, for example, Lidz et al's notion of 'pathological' families (1965) and the 'double-bind' hypothesis of Bateson et al (1956).

Around the same time as these 'causal' hypotheses were being promoted, the anti-psychotic drugs were discovered. Drugs, by their very nature, are treatments designated for the individual and this fact coupled with the prevailing view of families as toxic agents led, unsurprisingly, to what could cynically be called the first family intervention strategy – that of excluding the family.

C

    The family has played a central role in research into schizophrenia since the 1950s when, admittedly, the focus appeared to be on the family's role in the causation of the disorder. Consider, for example, Lidz et al's notion of 'pathological' families (1965) and the 'double-bind' hypothesis of Bateson et al (1956).
    Around the same time as these 'causal' hypotheses were being promoted, the anti-psychotic drugs were discovered. Drugs, by their very nature, are treatments designated for the individual and this fact coupled with the prevailing view of families as toxic agents led, unsurprisingly, to what could cynically be called the first family intervention strategy – that of excluding the family.

D

    The family has played a central role in research into schizophrenia since the 1950s when, admittedly, the focus appeared to be on the family's role in the causation of the disorder. Consider, for example, Lidz et al's notion of 'pathological' families (1965) and the 'double-bind' hypothesis of Bateson et al (1956).

    Around the same time as these 'causal' hypotheses were being promoted, the anti-psychotic drugs were discovered. Drugs, by their very nature, are treatments designated for the individual and this fact coupled with the prevailing view of families as toxic agents led, unsurprisingly, to what could cynically be called the first family intervention strategy – that of excluding the family.

CROSS REFERENCE

Chapter 2, Coherent texts and arguments, Cohesion and paragraph structure

Discussion: paragraph formatting

Most people find A difficult to read because the paragraphs are not clearly distinguished. B, C and D distinguish paragraphs in different ways: B has a line space between paragraphs; C starts each paragraph with an indentation. D uses both a line space and indentation. If there is indentation, the line space is not strictly necessary, but it does serve to make the distinction between paragraphs even clearer. It is very important that paragraphs are clearly distinguished. This ties in with the discussion in Chapter 2, where you saw how 'cohesive' paragraphs deal with a single, unified idea. Your formatting should underline this sense of cohesion.

Formatting tables and diagrams

It is important that tables and diagrams are labelled clearly and consistently. The examples below show the typical convention in academic writing, ie tables are labelled at the top, and diagrams are labelled at the bottom. If tables and diagrams are taken or adapted from other sources, they should be clearly referenced. The use of **bold** in labels should follow assessment guidelines; if this is not specified, just make sure you are consistent.

Example of a table:

Table 1: Treatments for depression according to patient group

Group	Treatment
1	Antidepressants
2	Problem-solving
3	Cognitive behavioural therapy
4	Physical exercise

Example of a figure:

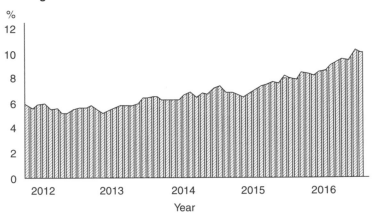

Figure 2: Percentage of patients in England waiting over 18 weeks for non-emergency treatment (Triggle, 2017)

If you have included tables and figures, make sure that you have referred to them clearly in the text, eg:

- As Table 1 shows/illustrates, …
- As can be seen in Table 1, …
- Figure 2 shows/illustrates …
- The RDA increases according to age (Table 1).
- Waiting times continue to rise (Figure 2).

Presentation

First impressions are important. The way your assignment looks says a lot about your approach to your studies. A well-presented piece of work shows that you are professional, pay attention to detail, and care about your work. It signals respect for the people who have set and will mark the assessment. It is not about decorating your work or making it striking to look at; it is about creating a document which is professional, clear and easy to navigate.

What should my essay look like?

1) It should have a title page

This should be the first sheet. Even if you are required to use a standard cover sheet for your assignments, there is no reason why you cannot also have a title page. You may be provided with guidelines on what to include, but if not, you may wish to include some or all of the following:

- your name (or your Student ID Number if the assignment is to be submitted anonymously, which it nearly always is nowadays);
- the institution for which it is being submitted, eg 'University of Towncaster – School of Nursing & Social Work';
- the title of the assignment;
- the course/module/programme for which it was written (including the date you commenced the course);
- the date of submission or the date you completed the assessment;
- your course unit leader's name and/or your academic adviser's name.

An example is given below:

The University of Towncaster
School of Nursing and Midwifery

BNurs (Hons)
(2017 Cohort)

NURS12053 Life Long Learning

Reflective Essay

Student: 0012345

Submission date: 6th October 2017

Course Unit Lead: Dr Colin Lead
Academic Adviser: Dr Ann Adviser

2) The word count should be written on the document

Make it very clear that you have met the word limit by writing the word count at the end of the document. In Microsoft Word, the word count of a document is clearly visible in the bottom left-hand corner of the screen.

3) Your pages should be numbered

If you or a lecturer prints out copies, it is very easy to get things in the wrong order if the pages are not secured together. In Microsoft Word, page numbers are added using the 'insert' tool on the toolbar. You can format these in a number of ways (eg bottom of the page, top of the page, centred, right-hand corner, left-hand corner). Experiment until you find a style that suits you, or that works well with a particular document.

4) It should be written using an appropriate font

Academic work should be written in a font which is easy to read and appropriately 'serious'. This may be specified in the guidelines. If not, use either:

- Times New Roman
- Arial

Inappropriate fonts include:

- Comic Sans

Comic Sans is a popular, 'friendly' font, but it tends to make documents look childish (which explains why it is used in many primary schools).

In Microsoft Word, font (and size – see below) can be easily selected from the toolbar.

5) The font size should be readable and appropriate

Don't use too large or too small a font size. A font size of 12pt is ideal; anything above font size 14pt will appear rather childish, and anything below 10pt will be far too small to read comfortably. Larger font sizes may be used for headings and subheadings. Again, this may be specified in the assessment guidelines.

6) It should look professional

Do not decorate your scripts with fancy pictures and colours. Aim for a professional look, rather than a decorative or striking one.

7) It should follow printing guidelines

Many universities now require you to submit your written assessments electronically, but on those occasions when you are required to print out hard copies, check guidelines on whether you should print on both sides or on one side only. You will often need to print out hard copies of documents for your **portfolio**.

And finally …

Finding advice and support

Universities provide a range of academic writing support. This goes by different names, including 'insessional classes', 'academic literacy support' and 'study skills', and will cover academic writing and other skills, such as speaking or critical thinking. The provision may distinguish between home students and international students, or it may be aimed at both sets of students. This type of integrated provision is becoming more common as it has been recognised that the most problematic issues in academic writing, such as coherence and style, affect all students, not just international students. Of course, students who speak English as a second language may also need specific English-language support, and many universities offer classes in areas such as grammar and pronunciation.

As well as academic writing classes, most universities have 'writing consultations', sometimes known as 'writing tutorials'. These involve meeting with an expert in English language and academic skills to discuss a piece of your writing. The length of these consultations varies, but they usually range from 30 minutes to an hour. You are usually required to send the work in advance. This could be an assignment for which you have already received a mark and feedback, or an assignment which you are currently working on. In the former case, the tutor will be able to help you understand why you received the mark and the feedback you did. In the latter case, the tutor will be able to give you advice on how to improve the piece of work before submission. In both cases, the real focus is not on that particular piece of work, but on you as a developing academic writer: it is a formative consultation rather than a proofreading service. The tutor may help you to correct some errors of grammar, punctuation and style, but they are more likely to focus on issues of clarity, coherence, style and readability. The advice you receive should help you develop your academic writing skills and apply these to future work. The fact that the tutor is very unlikely to be an expert in nursing is actually an advantage, as it will provide a test of whether your explanations of concepts and theories are accessible to a non-expert, as they should be. If you do want help with a piece of work in progress, make sure you leave enough time before submission, as it can take a few weeks to go through the university's booking system.

Summary

This chapter has guided you through the process of preparing your work for submission so as to meet the expectations of your lecturers at university. It has advised you on how to approach the final editing and proofreading process, and it has discussed the issues surrounding proofreading. It has provided you with information and guidance on formatting and presentation, and a presentation 'checklist' that you can apply to any piece of work before submitting it. Finally, it has offered advice on what you can do if you feel you need further professional support with your writing. You should now be ready to submit your writing for assessment, confident in the knowledge that you have done all you can to meet the expectations of your lecturers.

Sources of example texts

Ayhan, H, Iyigun, E, Ince, S, Can, M, Hatipoglu, S and Saglam, M (2015) A Randomised Clinical Trial Comparing the Patient Comfort and Efficacy of Three Different Graduated Compression Stockings in the Prevention of Postoperative Deep Vein Thrombosis. *Journal of Clinical Nursing*, 24, 2247–57.

Pryjmachuk, S (2011) The Capable Mental Health Nurse. In Pryjmachuk, S (ed) *Mental Health Nursing: An Evidence-Based Introduction*. London: Sage, 42–72.

Triggle, N (2017) NHS Operations: Waiting Times to Rise in 'Trade-off', Boss Says. *BBC News*, 31st March [online]. Available at: www.bbc.co.uk/news/health-39420662 (accessed 2 April 2017).

Appendix 1
English language references

This is not meant to be an exhaustive list of resources, but rather a selection of those that we think you may find most useful.

Dictionaries

There are many online dictionaries, but if you prefer to feel the weight of one in your hands, then Chambers is a good choice:

Chambers 21st Century Dictionary (1999) Edinburgh: Chambers Harrap Publishers Ltd.

A good online dictionary, especially for students whose first language is not English, is the Cambridge Dictionary. The definitions are very clear and easy to understand, and there is an excellent pronunciation tool:

Cambridge Dictionary [online]. Available at: http://dictionary.cambridge.org/ (accessed 26 March 2017).

Grammar books

Caplan, N (2012) *Grammar Choices for Graduate and Professional Writers*. Ann Arbor, MI: University of Michigan Press.

Caplan's book is aimed at postgraduate students (known as 'graduate' students in the USA, where this book is published). Nevertheless, if you are looking for a systematic analysis of English grammar in the context of academic English, you may find this book very useful. It contains many clear examples of grammar in use in real-life academic writing.

Hewings, M (2015) *Advanced Grammar in Use*. 3rd ed. Cambridge: Cambridge University Press.

Murphy, R (2015) *English Grammar in Use*. 4th ed. Cambridge: Cambridge University Press.

Murphy, R (2015) *Essential Grammar in Use*. 4th ed. Cambridge: Cambridge University Press.

The Grammar in Use series is particularly useful for students whose first language is not English. The books present each grammar point in a clear and systematic way, and provide exercises and a self-study answer key. There are also lots of multimedia features in recent editions.

Other resources

Academic Phrasebank. Available at: www.phrasebank.manchester.ac.uk/ (accessed 14 May 2017).

Academic Word List. Available at: www.victoria.ac.nz/lals/resources/academicwordlist (accessed 2 April 2017).

Baily, S (2011) *Academic Writing for International Students of English*. 3rd ed. Oxon: Routledge.

Bottomley, J (2014) *Academic Writing for International Students of Science*. Oxon: Routledge.

Peck, J and Cole, M (2012) *Write it Right: The Secrets of Effective Writing*. 2nd ed. New York: Palgrave Macmillan.

Swales, J and Feak, C (2012) *Academic Writing for Graduate Students: Essential Tasks and Skills*. 3rd ed. Michigan: Michigan ELT.

Appendix 2
Grammatical terminology

GRAMMATICAL TERM	DEFINITION	EXAMPLES
adjective	a word which describes a **noun**	an <u>elderly</u> woman a <u>diagnostic</u> test
adverb	a word which adds information to a **verb** or an **adjective**	inject <u>daily</u> a <u>very</u> large dose
article	the words 'a/an' and 'the', used with **nouns**	<u>a</u> bedpan <u>the</u> geriatric ward
clause	a structure containing a **verb**, forming a sentence, or joining with other clauses to form sentences	(1) <u>This essay aims to explore current treatments for malaria.</u> (1) <u>The women could not attend the clinic</u> (2) <u>because there was no public transport</u>. (1) <u>Founded in 1823,</u> (2) <u>the hospital has long provided health care for the local community.</u>
conjunction (linking word/phrase)	a word or phrase that joins words, phrases or **clauses**	food <u>and</u> water take once a day <u>but</u> only after a meal The women could not attend the clinic (main clause) <u>because</u> there was no public transport (subordinate clause). <u>If</u> symptoms persist (subordinate clause), a course of antibiotics may be required (main clause).
contraction	two words joined by an apostrophe	<u>he's</u> in ward 5 <u>it's</u> 4pm
countable noun*	a **noun** which can be counted and so can be used in the **plural**	a <u>midwife</u>, <u>midwives</u> the <u>patient</u>, the <u>patients</u>
main clause	the **clause** containing the main idea in a **sentence**	<u>This essay aims to explore current treatments for malaria.</u> <u>The women could not attend the clinic</u> because there was no public transport. Founded in 1823, <u>the hospital has long provided health care for the local community.</u> <u>The study suggests</u> that this is a promising treatment.
noun	people, places or things	child, hospital, duty, training

GRAMMATICAL TERM	DEFINITION	EXAMPLES
participle clause	a **clause** with an '–ing' or '–ed' verb form adding information to the **main clause**	<u>Founded in 1823</u>, the hospital has long provided health care for the local community. The study investigated the effects of chronic illness on families, <u>using mixed methods research</u>.
plural	the form of a **noun** that refers to more than one, usually ending in 's' in English	drugs, nurses, babies women, children, criteria (irregular plurals)
possessive	a word or phrase which denotes belonging	<u>her</u> child <u>Mrs Brown's</u> child the child is <u>hers</u>
proper noun	a noun written with a capital letter, as it is the name of a person, place, company etc	Fatima, London, Mind, NICE, Pfizer
sentence	a group of words usually beginning with a capital letter and ending in a full stop, and containing a **subject** and a **verb**; the main building blocks of writing	Students are advised to make an appointment with their academic adviser. This essay aims to explore current treatments for malaria. The women could not attend the clinic because there was no public transport. Founded in 1823, the hospital has long provided health care for the local community. The study suggests that this is a promising treatment.
singular	the form of a **noun** that refers to one of something	a ward the doctor
subject	the person or thing which the **verb** relates to and agrees with in number	<u>Students</u> are advised to make an appointment with their academic adviser. <u>The study</u> suggests that this is a promising treatment.
that-clause	a **subject/verb** structure that follows certain verbs etc that are usually followed by 'that'	The study suggests <u>that this is a promising treatment</u>.
uncountable noun*	a **noun** seen as a mass which cannot be split or counted, and so cannot be **plural**	pain, time, energy, sugar, cancer
quantifier	a word or phrase which denotes 'how much' of a **noun**	<u>few</u> people <u>a large amount of</u> money

GRAMMATICAL TERM	DEFINITION	EXAMPLES
verb	a word expressing an action or state	be, have, go, wash, eat, treat, inject, administer Students <u>are</u> advised to make an appointment with their academic adviser. The study <u>suggests</u> that this is a promising treatment.

*This is often about how a noun is interpreted in a particular context, rather than an absolute concept. Many nouns can be countable or uncountable depending on the context, eg:

research into **cancer**

many **cancers** can be treated with chemotherapy

nurses can administer **medicine**

a new **medicine**

Appendix 3
Key phrases in assignments

PHRASE	LEVEL	MEANING
analyse	Mostly Levels 5 and 6, especially with the word 'critically'; rarely Level 4	Look at the concepts and ideas under discussion in depth; the addition of 'critically' means look at the concepts and ideas in depth **and** with a critical eye
assess	All levels, though common at lower levels	Make comments about the value/importance of the concepts and ideas under discussion
compare	All levels, though common at lower levels	Look for similarities between the concepts and ideas under discussion
contrast	All levels, though common at lower levels	Look for differences between the concepts and ideas under discussion; often used with 'compare' (see above)
define	All levels, though common at lower levels	State precisely what is meant by a particular issue, theory or concept
discuss	Level 5 and above; sometimes Level 4	Give reasons for and against; investigate and examine by argument
evaluate	Mostly Levels 5 and 6, especially with the word 'critically'	Weigh up the arguments surrounding an issue, using your own opinions and, more importantly, reference to the work of others
illustrate	All levels	Make clear by the use of examples
outline	All levels, though tends to be used with the lower levels	Give the main features of
review	All levels, though 'critically review' would imply Level 5 and above	Extract relevant information from a document or set of documents
state	All levels, though tends to be used with the lower levels	Present in a clear, concise form
summarise	All levels, though tends to be used with the lower levels	Give an account of all the main points of the concepts and ideas under discussion
with reference to	All levels	Use a specific context, issue or concept to make the meaning clear

Appendix 4
Academic levels at university

UNDERGRADUATE STUDY			
England, Wales, Northern Ireland	**Scotland**	**Award**	**Notes**
Level 4	Level 7	Certificate of Higher Education (CertHE)	
Level 5	Level 8	Diploma of Higher Education (DipHE) Foundation Degree (FdD)	Up until 2010, minimum academic qualification for nurses
Level 6	Level 9	Ordinary Bachelor Degree eg BSc Nursing	Minimum academic qualification for nurses and midwives; common exit point in Scotland
	Level 10	Bachelor Degree with Honours eg BSc (Hons) in Nursing Studies, BNurs (Hons), BMidwif (Hons)	Usual academic qualification for nurses and midwives in England, Wales and Northern Ireland
POSTGRADUATE STUDY			
Level 7	Level 11	Masters Degree, eg MSc, MA, MPhil Postgraduate Certificate or Diploma (PGCert; PGDip)	Minimum academic qualification for Advanced Practitioners
Level 8	Level 12	Research Doctorate (PhD) Professional Doctorate eg DNurs, MD, ClinPsychD	Recommended qualification for Advanced Practitioners who are Nurse Consultants

Answer key

Chapter 1

Reflective essays, Task

A   Description of a situation and feelings

B   Analysis of feelings

C/D Action taken at the time, exploration of the issues, resulting outcomes, understanding achieved, future action identified

Chapter 2

Organisational frameworks, Task

1)

A Classification: factors affecting individual's health, exemplification

B Classification: 1) how we communicate, 2) who we communicate to

C Problem-solution: ways of tackling alcohol misuse

D Classification: responses to HIV diagnosis – perhaps chronological stages

E Cause-effect (reasons for drop in applications) and problem-solution

F Compares and contrasts alternative viewpoints in the literature

2)

A

Introduction/background – refer to title

- Definition of health
- Factors influencing an individual's health (diet, environment, lifestyle, socio-economic status, cultural factors)
- Extent to which nurses can influence
- compare with influence of other health professionals, eg doctors
- Concept of 'empowerment'
- Contextualise to my field of nursing

Conclusion – can have an impact, but other factors (eg clean water, cessation of smoking) have more – potential of nurses to influence these things?

B

Introduction/background – claimed that communication is the <u>core</u> skill of nursing

- Definition of communication
- Different types of communication: verbal, written, non-verbal
- Different forms of communication: patients, families, colleagues, partner organisations
- Relative importance of (other) different core skills (NMC): leadership, intellectual skills, admin skills, clinical skills – less important than communication?
- How communication impacts on other aspects of nursing – thus more important?
- Problems caused by breakdown in communication (eg Francis report)

Conclusion – nurses need a range of skills but communication is integral to all, and very difficult to be a good nurse without good communication skills, even if competent in 'technical' skills

General and specific information, Task

General: What does managing the delivery of health and social care involve?

Managing the delivery of health and social care in the UK involves collaborating with a variety of complex organisations and professionals within a diverse workforce.

Specific: problem

Nowadays, healthcare staff are constantly under pressure to improve services often when resources are stretched.

Specific: consequence

In certain circumstances this can result in a communication breakdown or poor provision of care which leads to frustration, particularly when this involves patients and relatives who may be anxious and upset, distressed or angry.

Specific: what it means for you as a nurse

Therefore it is somewhat inevitable that you will encounter difficult situations at some stage in your career.

Old and new information, Task

Phrases in **bold** refer back to information underlined

Patients and service users are being encouraged to take more control of their own care (Department of Health, 2009) and they have an important part to play in determining how services are designed, implemented and evaluated (The Kings Fund, 2012). By collaborating with service users and responding appropriately to their feedback, nurses can deliver more appropriate care and ensure that any concerns raised are dealt with quickly and appropriately (Coulter, 2012). **This** will usually involve collecting and using information provided by patients (e.g. patient satisfaction surveys or focus groups) in order to deliver the kind of services that patients want. **Whichever approach** is used, the key aim is to find out what patients really think about the services we provide and provide supporting evidence of **this**.

Noun or pronoun?, Task

Fatigue is commonly experienced by people suffering from a variety of chronic illnesses. In the sixteenth century, the concept of fatigue was related to a tedious duty; nowadays, fatigue is understood as a state of feeling tired for 'no reason'; Barsevick et al. (2010) define it as a subjective state, a feeling unrelated to that of being tired after exercise or relieved after rest. It may be regarded as exhaustive, unpredictable in its course, and affecting cognitive ability. Fatigue is often described as multidimensional and disabling, affecting the quality of life of those living with it. It is associated with negative emotions such as anxiety, numbness and vulnerability. These are likely to impact on social relationships and family life, often leading to withdrawal and social isolation.

Notes

Other combinations are possible; the important thing to remember is to avoid ambiguity and to be sensitive to the reader's need to be reminded of the topic frequently.

Referring back in the text to summarise and comment, Task

1) 'This important aspect of mental health'

2)

a) This case

b) This view

c) this serious problem

d) Whichever approach

e) Whichever treatment

f) This disease

3)

a) health promotion

b) these Acts (could also be 'this legislation')

c) these areas

d) This ability to self-govern our behaviours

Linking ideas, Task

1)

a) In addition (it is an additional point, but not a more important one)

b) In contrast ('on the contrary' contradicts a negative or a question, eg 'He is not fit to work. On the contrary, he has a serious condition which requires total rest.'

c) albeit (has the same meaning as 'although' but is used before noun/adjective/adverb phrases, not subjects and verbs)

d) whereby ('a process whereby' is a common phrase)

e) thereby (usually followed by –ing; 'hereby' is usually only used in very formal phrases such as 'I hereby pronounce you …')

f) namely ('in other words', precedes an explanation of what has just been said)

g) respectively (refers back to two things in the same order)

h) the former, the latter (very useful for referring back precisely)

2)

Asthma is a chronic inflammatory disease of the respiratory system. ~~Furthermore~~, it is episodic in nature and variable in severity. ~~However~~, it affects people of all ages. ~~Given that~~ it is ~~also~~ most commonly caused by heightened responsiveness to allergen triggers, resulting in inflammation and narrowing of the airways in affected individuals. ~~While~~ it has been recommended that patients should be fully involved in decisions regarding their treatment. However, a survey conducted by Asthma UK reported that 50% of sufferers had not had a full discussion with a health professional.

Chapter 3

Referencing errors, Task

1)

a) There is no publication year, which name-year (Harvard) systems require:

> According to Tarrier and Barrowclough (1996), carers need information, and professionals have a moral duty to supply it.

b) This citation is information-prominent. Both the name and the date should be in brackets, and at the end of the sentence and before the full stop:

> The major hindrance appears to be the cultural dominance of 'technical rationality' (Schön, 1988).

c) Alphabetical sequencing is required to distinguish between two publications in the same year:

In a theoretical paper, Dickoff and James (1968a) argue this position, which is subsequently backed up by a further, data-based paper (Dickoff and James, 1968b).

d) Round, rather than square, brackets are the norm:

Meleis (2001) speculates that historical and cultural paternalism are largely to blame.

e) This citation is a direct quote so the quote must be enclosed in speech marks and the page number must be provided. Since it's a quote that actively involves the author's name, the year needs to be in brackets:

To quote from Benner (1984): 'Expertise develops when the clinician tests and refines propositions, hypotheses and principle-based expectations in actual practice situations' (p 37).

Alternatively:

To quote from Benner (1984, p 37): 'Expertise develops when the clinician tests and refines propositions, hypotheses and principle-based expectations in actual practice situations.'

f) The authors' initials are not required in the main body of text* (only the final reference list):

According to Green (2008) women are the primary carers in society.

* There is an exception when you have authors with the same surname who have published in the same year and you want to distinguish between them in your work. For example, if you had used a book by Mary Green from 2008 and also one by Helen Green from 2008, you'd refer to the first as M Green (2008) and the second as H Green (2008).

g) With two or more authors, you use 'et al' in the main body of text (but list all authors in the final reference list):

The results are consistent with the findings of Posner et al (2012).

h) Round brackets are required rather than square ones, and there is no year for Smith:

Smith (1989, cited by Jones 1992) suggests that the findings are incomplete.

i) The following is more academic:

… (see, for example, the 'change spiral' of Lewin, 1958).

j) The citation actively involves the author (is author-prominent) so the brackets need to go round the year only:

Schon (1988) suggests that this paradox can be resolved by acknowledging the importance of subjectivity.

2)

Note that there may be slight variations in styles across publishers and departments.

a) Smith, R W (1996) *Psychology and Health Care*. London: Ballère Tindall.

b) Weleminsky, J (1991) Schizophrenia and the Family: The Customers' View. *International Review of Psychiatry*, 3, 119–24.

c) Stevens, B J (1984) *Nursing Theory: Analysis, Application and Evaluation*. 2nd ed. Philadelphia: Lippincott.

d) Richards, D, Bee, P, Loftus, S, Bakerm J, Bailey, L and Lovell, K (2005) Specialist Educational Intervention for Acute Inpatient Mental Health Nursing Staff: Service User Views and Effects on Nursing Quality. *Journal of Advanced Nursing*, 51, 634–44.

e) Lindsay, B (1991) The Gap between Theory and Practice. *Nursing Standard*, 5(4), 34–35.

f) Calman, K C and Royston, G (1997) Risk Language and Dialects. *British Medical Journal*, 315, 939–42.

g) Social Exclusion Unit (2002) *Reducing Re-offending by Ex-prisoners*. London: Social Exclusion Unit.

h) Parsonage, M, Fossey, M and Tutty, C (2012) *Liaison Psychiatry in the Modern NHS*. London: Centre for Mental Health. Available at: www.centreformentalhealth.org.uk/liaison-psychiatry-nhs (accessed 14 May 2017).

Focus, Task

1)

Information-prominent: b, d, f

Author-prominent: a, c, e

2)

a) <u>As</u> Wright (1993) <u>points out</u>, one of the paradoxes of successful change is that it escapes public notice simply because it is successful.

c) <u>According to</u> Scheidlinger and Aronson (2001), group therapy has been used to treat a wide range of symptomolotalogy in adolescents.

e) Thomas et al (2013) <u>argue that</u> nursing will only really develop as a profession if nurses become more political.

3)

a) advocate

b) identify/identified

c) acknowledge

d) distinguishes between

e) argues that

f) define Diabetes Mellitus as

Chapter 4

Being concise, Task

Square brackets, eg [the country of] = unnecessary

Strike through, eg ~~and learned about~~ = definitely needs to be deleted (completely redundant or 'tautological', or extremely wordy)

Mary Seacole was born in [the country of] Jamaica in [the year] 1805. She studied ~~and learned about~~ herbal medicine in ~~the country of~~ Jamaica. She was also well travelled, and during her travels ~~to different places~~, she acquired a great deal of knowledge on medicine ~~and drugs~~ and caring for the sick. Like her contemporary ~~of the same time~~, Florence Nightingale, she petitioned people in the British government to send her to Crimea to help ~~and assist~~ in the ~~army~~ military hospital. The ~~country's~~ government declined her request, but she decided to fund her own visit ~~by herself with her own money~~. In Crimea, she nursed sick and wounded soldiers. Seacole died in the year 1910. Her contribution to medicine went unrecognised while she was alive but, in 1991, she was posthumously awarded the Jamaican Order of Merit ~~after her death~~, and in 2004, she came top of a poll to decide the 'greatest black Briton'. She is considered by many people to be a pioneer of nursing.

Notes

'in the country of' is OK the first time you introduce it, but not subsequently

'sick' and 'wounded' describe different things so this is not redundancy

'the year 1910' emphasises the year; here we want to emphasise what happened

'contemporary' contains the meaning 'at the same time' – combining them creates a tautology; the same with 'posthumously' and 'after her death'

Being precise, Task

1) evolved
2) invasive
3) determine
4) exhibiting
5) administer
6) diagnostic
7) in terms of
8) associated with

Identifying inappropriate language, Task

1) male/man/~~bloke~~
2) inebriated/~~tipsy~~/drunk
3) ~~impecunious~~/poor/~~broke~~
4) food/nutrition/~~grub~~
5) sleep/~~slumber~~/~~doze~~

Identifying formal language, Task

1) Little
2) deteriorated
3) was awarded
4) approximately
5) adhere; enshrined within
6) demonstrate
7) ensure
8) such as
9) improve
10) facilitate
11) An increasing number of
12) many

Improving style, Task

The aging population means that **an increasing number of** people have to be carers and **many** of them are struggling. They often **do not receive** help and **they are** facing cuts in the benefits and services they **are entitled to. A number of studies have reported that** that the general health of carers **deteriorates** the more hours of care they **provide. A positive** partnership with professionals will **greatly improve** outcomes for both carers and patients. All professionals, **including** doctors, district nurses, **and** general practice nurses, should respect carers as expert partners in care. **Furthermore,** community nurses need to have certain values and skills, **such as** compassion, competence, commitment, to make sure carers' health and wellbeing is looked after.

Commonly confused words, Task

1) practice
2) practise
3) advice
4) advise
5) device
6) devised
7) licensed
8) licence
9) effects
10) affected
11) their
12) There

Variation in comma use, Task

B separates phrases and clauses using commas; A does not. It is arguably easier for the reader to have these commas. A could have three commas:

> The assessment of a person's capacity to give or withhold consent is considered in relation to a specific decision. While the individual may not have capacity to make some decisions, they may still retain capacity for other decisions. For example, a patient may not have capacity to make a decision regarding a surgical procedure, but could retain capacity to consent (or not) to having their clinical observations (e.g. blood pressure) checked.

Grammar and punctuation, Task

1)

Social factors also seem to influence depression rates. Depression is more common in the unemployed, those living alone, those who are divorced or separated, those living in local authority or housing association accommodation, those with a lower socioeconomic status and/or material disadvantage, and those with no formal educational qualifications. Social factors such as isolation, racist attacks and dissatisfaction with housing may also contribute to depression in refugee groups. Indeed, in traumatised refugees and asylum seekers, poor social support seems to be a stronger predictor of depression in the long term than the severity of the initial trauma.

2)

Postnatal depression affects 10–15 in every 100 women after childbirth. It can be difficult to detect because it may present differently in different women. The symptoms of postnatal depression are similar to those of depression at any other stage of life; the difference is the presence of a baby, which is likely to be the focus of the woman's thoughts and difficulties. The disorder may be mild or severe. Milder forms might be treated within the primary healthcare team, while more severe forms will require additional input from psychiatric services. Diagnosing postnatal depression requires clinical assessment by a GP or mental health specialist. However, nursing and midwifery staff must be alert to the disorder in order make timely referrals.

Parallel structures, Task

1)

Medication errors can impact on patients, nurses and organisations.
Or
Medication errors can impact on all stakeholders: patients, nurses and organisations.

2)

One initiative which aims to help vulnerable young first-time mothers across the UK is the Family Nurse Partnership Programme (FNP). This programme aims to:

- improve pregnancy outcomes;
- improve child health and development;
- improve parents' economic self-sufficiency.

(Taylor, 2015, p 141)

Or

One initiative which aims to help vulnerable young first-time mothers across the UK is the Family Nurse Partnership Programme (FNP). This programme aims to: improve pregnancy outcomes; improve child health and development; and improve parents' economic self-sufficiency.

Or

One initiative which aims to help vulnerable young first-time mothers across the UK is the Family Nurse Partnership Programme (FNP). This programme aims to improve pregnancy outcomes, child health and development, and parents' economic self-sufficiency.

3)

Some elderly patients remain mobile through activities such as driving or playing golf; others are largely sedentary, spending a lot of time indoors reading or watching TV.

Or

Some elderly patients remain mobile; others are largely sedentary. The former group stay mobile through activities such as driving or playing golf; the latter group spend a lot of time indoors reading or watching TV.

4)

Standing (2010) has identified three main theories which underpin the decision-making process in nursing: normative, descriptive, and prescriptive.

Chapter 5

Proofreading practice, Task

A

Female hormones are implicated in a number of cancers. The contraceptive pill contains a low dose of the hormone oestrogen, which is linked with breast and cervical cancer. However, they also contain progesterone, which is known to be protective against endometrial cancer. According to the NHS, the risks associated with the pill are relatively small for most women and its benefits outweigh the risks. There are, however, a number of women who are more at risk, including those over 35, smokers, and those with high blood pressure.

B

Of central importance to cognitive psychologists is the 'schema' notion. A schema is a mental 'template' that guides behaviour or thought, in a similar way that a recipe is a template for creating an exotic dish (Schemata actually guide external and external action, external action being observable behaviour, internal action being thought.) Any action, internal or external, will have a schema underpinning it.

Thus, there are schemata for skilled tasks, like driving or typing, schemata for making judgements about people, schemata for language, schemata for perceiving, and so on. Some aspects of certain schemata may be inherited (indeed, the simplest schemata are mere reflex actions); the vast majority are acquired. To those familiar with computers, a schema is little more than the software that drives our action. However, unlike computer software, schemata can replicate, change and become redundant as we experience the world.

Schemata help us process the vast amount of information in the world. They serve us well for the majority of the time; however, they are not always applicable to a particular situation and when we misapply them, errors occur. For example, when we misapply a 'braking' schema whilst driving, we might be involved in an accident. Similarly, the misapplication of 'judgemental' schemata can lead to the creation of stereotypes.

Index